AMERICA

AMERICA
–A REDISCOVERY–

LANCE MORROW

HENRY HOLT AND COMPANY
NEW YORK

Published in the United States by
Henry Holt and Company, Inc., 521 Fifth Avenue,
New York, New York 10175.

Originally published in Canada by
Key Porter Books Limited, Toronto

Library of Congress Catalog Card Number 87-80677

ISBN: 0-8050-0584-6

First American Edition

Design: Peggy Heath and Associates
Typesetting: Compeer Typographic Services Ltd
Printed and bound in Italy

10 9 8 7 6 5 4 3 2 1

ISBN 0-8050-0584-6

Page 1: *A rolling celebration of America's bicentennial in 1976.*

Page 2: *A New England landscape: mist clears on Peacham, Vermont.*

Page 3: *The rim of the Grand Canyon is in places more than 6,000 feet above the Colorado River.*

This page: *Baseball, the all-American game, is part sport and part myth.*

Opposite page: *The White House, the official residence of the President and his family, has become a symbol of the United States around the world.*

Following pages: *The palm trees and skyscrapers of Los Angeles light up for the night. The city and its environs are home to over nine million Americans.*

PHOTO CREDITS

Picture research and selection by Joan Tedeschi.
All photographs provided by Image Bank from the following photographers (number indicates the page on which the photograph appears):

Morton Beebe: 64–65, 227; Derek Berwin: 167 (top); Tim Bieber: 172; Ira Block: 98 (bottom), 152 (top); Ernest Braun: 224; Gerald Brimacombe: 13, 168, 207 (bottom); Donald E. Carroll: 232–233; Bill Carter: 67; Luis Castaneda: 42; Andy Caulfield: 21, 40–41, 196 (bottom); Flip Chalfant: 26 (bottom), 230 (bottom); Kathleen Norris Cook: 3, 228–229; Lisl Dennis: 144 (top); Yuri Dojc: 199; Steve Dunwell: 8, 70 (top), 94, 166, 222 (bottom), 237 (top); Robert V. Eckert, Jr.: 213 (bottom); Faustino: 120–121; Nicholas Foster: 216, 239; Jay Freis: 158 (top), 205, 207 (top); Lawrence Fried: 145, 170, 235; Brett Froomer: 6–7, 46 (bottom), 230 (top); Daniel Forer: 126–127; G & J Images: 125 (top), 176 (bottom); Garry Gay: 203; Bob Gelberg: 210 (top), 217 (top); Gary Gladstone: 171 (bottom); Larry Dale Gordon: 123; Geoffrey Gove: 44–45, 152 (top), 154–155; Farrell Grehan: 158 (bottom); David William Hamilton: 48, 63, 66 (right), 71 (right), 159 (bottom), 174–175, 237 (bottom); Gregory Heisler: 157; Karl Hentz: 34–35; Eddie Hironaka: 88–89; David Hiser: 147, 171 (top); Walter Iooss, Jr.: 4, 30; Janeart Ltd.: 31, 118, 139, 153, 162, 206; Lou Jones: 196 (top); Ted Kawalerski: 47; John Kelly: 161 (bottom), 167, 223; Tom King: 213 (top); Douglas Kirkland: 125 (bottom); Steve Krongard: 25; Donald Landwehrle: 22–23; Whitney Lane: 159 (top); Robert Latorre: 33; William Logan: 37; Bullaty/Lomeo: 36 (right); David J. Maenza: 167 (bottom); Richard & Mary Magruder: 92 (left); Jay Maisel: cover, 46 (top); Joanna McCarthy: 93; Tom McCarthy: 87, 160 (bottom); Patti McConville: 70 (bottom); Burton McNeely: 100; Peter Miller: 2, 96–97, 99, 128 (top), 151; Benn Mitchell: 160 (top); Toby Molenaar: 119 (bottom); David Muench: 178, 194–195; Marvin E. Newman: 5, 140–141, 142, 150; George Obremski: 32 (bottom), 119 (top); Robert Ostrowski: 222 (top); Robert Phillips: 143, 164; Charles Place: 39 (bottom); Steve Proehl: 198, 212; Jake Rajs: 72, 117, 173, 225 (top); Marc Reto: 176 (top); Co Rentmeester: 28–29; Fulvio Roiter: 144 (bottom); Barrie Rokeach: 220–221; Marc Romanelli: 24, 36 (left), 98 (top); Peter Runyon: 124, 234; Ted Russell: 202; Michael Salas: 128 (bottom); Al Satterwhite: 91 (bottom), 231; Michael Schneps: 26 (top), 39 (top); Gerhard Gscheidle: 148–149; Allan Seiden: 71 (left); Ivor Sharp: 130; Jeff Smith: 211; Marc Solomon: 32 (top), 236; John Lewis Stage: 114–115, 116, 129, 200–201, 204; Alex Stewart: 91 (top), 219; Stockphotos Inc.: 68–69, 226; Lynn M. Stone: 90; Harald Sund: 161 (top), 165 (bottom), 177, 197, 208–209, 214–215, 218, 225 (top); Pete Turner: 1, 30 (right), 210 (bottom); Alvis Upitis: 43, 146; Richard Ustinich: 38; Santi Visalli: 165 (top); Hans Wendler: 95, 217 (bottom); Frank Whitney: 193; A.T. Willett: 156; Art Wolfe: 238; Pamela J. Zilly: 66 (left), 92 (left)

CONTENTS

—AMERICAN PATCHWORK—

New York's 42nd Street has a pulse of nervous energy and a shimmer of the illicit.

There is no unity in the American landscape. The country is diverse and patchwork, like its immigration. America is an ingathering of mountain and desert and swamp and north woods and great plain.

Too much of the country now looks like the outskirts of Albuquerque — bright commercial highway strips of fast-food franchises and gas stations. They are loud and transient and depressing — depressing not because they are vulgar but because one feels their impermanence, their lack of connection.

Still, America has a thousand styles of landscape that cannot be ruined, or not for a long time. The American sense of place remains intact. America is an event of astonishing physical variety, and energy.

I find many American landscapes haunting in a way that puzzles me. The country is deeply resonant and full of histories. Yet, the human scratches upon the surface of the land have been so shallow, so passing. As one flies over America, one is amazed by how much of it is empty, unused.

My own taste in American landscape is eccentric. I love Kansas for reasons mystic and sentimental. The American prairie has an austere emptiness with subtleties of spiritual meaning not to be achieved in, say, the ecstatic Ektachromes of Hawaii. Northern Alabama is rough, lovely territory — small mountains and lakes as clear as the local moonshine they call Cat, for wildcat whiskey. The Big Bend country of Texas is a magic realm through which my great grandfather, a colonel of the Ninth Cavalry, chased a Mescalero Apache renegade named Victorio for many weeks more than a hundred years ago. Colonel Morrow lost Victorio there among the Mountains of the Moon. I love the upper peninsula of Michigan, the Florida Keys and the sweet rectilinear farmland of Indiana.

New York City, where I live, is a form of antinature. It exaggerates one side of the American impulse. The city looks sometimes as if nature had been grabbed by its hair — by its grass and trees — and uprooted, and then planted upside down, the sharp geometries of earth's underside, its crystals and ores, now torn out and stuck into the air. Here and elsewhere, Americans scalped the earth and planted their ambitions in it, so that the crystals of their ideas would grow up into the sunshine in sharp bright aggressive mental forms, intellectual blades. New York is a stabbing sort of city.

The Chrysler Building fires up out of the earth that way. It is to me a mysterious and beautiful building, a sort of pagan cathedral, vatic. Beneath the building lie subway tracks and then, down deeper, electric cables and sewer pipes and stones and, deeper still, old Indian camp fires and pots and arrowheads and fossils. Laminations of time.

In the late afternoon I walk along East Forty-fourth Street toward the subway (the building's needle spire points into sky, and I head down into the hole in the ground, the iron mole's run). Before I go into the earth, I see the startling Art Deco diadem. A cathedral and a mystery, but one that is tended now by secretaries and advertising executives.

At night, I may turn a corner and see the diadem set with its bright diamonds of light. The building is empty. There is a full moon, but the building's elegant effect makes the moon look somehow unfinished, like an uncut gem.

America, said E.M. Forster, the British novelist, is like life because "you usually find in it what you look for." In dark Prague, Franz Kafka imagined his *Amerika*. He believed that everyone there, always, invariably, was smiling.

There are as many Americas as there are minds to imagine America. America is an invented country, a creation of the mind. Alexis de Tocqueville, the French writer who visited the United States in 1831, said that it was "*une feuille blanche*," a blank page upon which history waited to be written. It is a country peopled by what sometimes now seems a smug gamble of the Enlightenment — an assumption of inevitable rational progress toward the light, an assumption that a government made holy by the Constitution (that American Ark of the Covenant) could turn one generation's conscious purposes into a timeless principle.

Japan, to name an opposite, took form from its Shinto mists, before history, before consciousness. The Japanese live, body and soul, in the place that has always been their home. Their life and culture arose organically over many centuries in the confines of their islands. The Japanese exist where they have always existed.

But Americans arrived from elsewhere, arrived across great distances, propelled by will and hope, greed and luck. Except for the native peoples, who were here when the whites arrived and were overwhelmed by them, Americans have by definition been immigrants: strivers and strangers. The African blacks were doubly strangers, since they arrived in chains. But they were immigrants nonetheless. America was consciously peopled. It was a continent not given but taken. Or rather the land was given, but it was wild. It had to be seized and subdued.

Everyone in the world is, of course, an immigrant in time, passing into the future. The immigrant who travels in both time and geographical space achieves another and more interesting dimension, that aroused by motion and change, by things happening. Humanity is no longer passive, no longer rooted. The dimensions of time and space collaborate. America, a place, becomes a time: the future.

Geographical space in America fulfills the role that time serves in other cultures. Other cultures, rooted in the same place, have spread out over time. America, rooted in a short time, a short history, spread out over space.

Much of American culture seems brightly purposeless. It is a strange business that a people as morally self-conscious as Americans, so much given to thinking about their ''national purpose,'' should have produced the bizarre gush of American popular culture: MTV and rock and Rambo and Monroe and Presley, snake handling and religious theme parks,

Dallas and *Dynasty,* Batman and the Flintstones and Coke and the Big Mac, the global culture of seductive junk. Much of the American energy is laissez-faire gone surreal. The Americans have a high seriousness about their meaning in the world (democracy, freedom, "the last best hope of man," as Lincoln said), but they express themselves as a sort of imperialist sugar shock — soda pop and Hollywood and bricks of pink bubble gum.

An image: a sort of rocket's gantry stands enigmatically beside the Hollywood sign that presides over the world capital of illusions, the city where the actor president of the United States, elected twice by handsome margins, learned to make American dreams look just like reality, interchangeable with reality, to the point that the president sometimes recited anecdotes from movies, heroic lore from combat films, as if they had actually occurred. On the other hand, America should not be understood too quickly.

One night in December 1972, NASA aimed its Apollo 17 rocket at the moon. It was to be the last shot of the Apollo series and the only one launched at night.

Richard Nixon had just been reelected president by the largest plurality in American history. He was five months past the Watergate burglary and twenty-one months from his resignation.

I flew to Cape Canaveral to watch the launch and sat with a crowd of other writers and journalists on a grassy field across a lagoon from the launchpad. There were many delays, all of them explained to us over loudspeakers in the flat and nerveless tones of the NASA "communicator."

Kurt Vonnegut, Jr., reclined on the grass and endlessly smoked cigarettes. Several hundred of us lounged in clusters, talking quietly, groaning a little when the disembodied baritone announced another delay. It was as if an airport waiting room had been edgily combined with a nighttime country picnic.

The voice of NASA expresses a kind of America, low-key, self-confident, holding in reserve a world of competence, and implied power, even lethal power. It is the style of American manhood exemplified by Gary Cooper. Except that now, at NASA, it has been carried over into an intricacy of technological teamwork and facelessness that contradicts the old individualism.

Across the lagoon, the Apollo moon rocket stood. A dozen searchlight beams of scorching intensity were aimed up at the white rocket. It stood in a cathedral of radiant light in the midst of the swampish subtropical Florida darkness.

In a way the rocket was the perfect American product, the perfect expression of American aspiration and cunning and teamwork. The capsule at the tip of the thing, where the astronauts Ron Evans, Jack Schmitt and Gene Cernan sat and waited, was the end of a line that was first drawn by the Greeks. We were counting down. "All is number," taught Pythagoras. The countdown passed through centuries and through the tinkering American minds of Orville and Wilbur Wright, numbers conspiring toward this rocket poised to fire up into the night.

The geometries of white light surrounding the rocket made me think of Hitler's 1934 Nuremberg rallies, which Leni Riefenstahl filmed in *Triumph of the Will*. A hieratic light, spooky and pagan — a rite of power. But the light show at Nuremberg dramatized the century's descent into darkness. The cathedral of light at Canaveral was an accidental and transient poetry. You were not supposed to notice. The purpose at hand was to send some men to the moon. That thought was perfectly American: do not be distracted by the symbolism. Keep your eye on the ball. Later, Ronald Reagan's America passed through that looking glass and the symbolism mastered the substance.

The rocket had been literally dug out of the earth by Americans — well, by Americans and (although one did not like to dwell upon it) certain German rocket scientists who made their way across the ocean after the V-2 rocket works at Peenemünde shut down. Americans had brought up the earth's ores and minerals and then fired them and fashioned them and machined them and measured them and twisted them and assembled them into this. They had done what Americans do best: they had transformed nature into power they could use.

The building of the rocket replicated the process by which the ingathering of people from all over the world had assaulted nature in America and transformed it into a vehicle that would lift it from the past and thrust it into the future. In 1879, in celebration of the first hundred years of the U.S. Constitution, James Russell Lowell, the nineteenth-century poet and editor, said, "After our Constitution got fairly into working order, it really seemed as if we had invented a machine that would go of itself, and this begot a faith in our luck."

At length, Kurt Vonnegut and the rest of us stood up. The flat American voice on the loudspeaker was counting backward.

At zero, the base of the cathedral erupted in spumes of white vapor that billowed outward. Then came a hard, downward mass of yellow flame, and then, belatedly, to our ears, the blat-blat-blat-blatting racket, a stuttering thunder, then the roar. And then, in a dreamlike slow motion, the great white rocket rose out of its cathedral of light into the darkness. The earth beneath us now trembled rapidly in rhythm with the blatting rockets, and we watched the Apollo gathering strength, winning against gravity, trailing its hard yellow fire beneath it until, long seconds later, the yellow light diminishing, it dopplered into the upper atmosphere.

Left behind, we all grinned and ran our fingers through our hair in a rapid mussing motion. Vladimir Nabokov, the novelist, once said that a line of great poetry always caused him to do that: leap up and run his fingers through his hair.

The Cadillac hurtled down the four-lane highway through the Alabama darkness, after midnight, south from Scottsboro to Montgomery. A man named Guido Roncallo was driving. George Wallace, Jr., son of the former governor, sat in the front passenger seat, and I in the back.

No other cars were on the road. Guido held the Cadillac at a smooth eighty miles per hour, twenty-five miles per hour over the legal speed limit. Our headlights glared down the highway, which was margined with stands of oak and cedar and tall pine.

The trees were the stately primal growth, with their origins back beyond the days of slavery, I imagined, and they were robed in kudzu, the dense wild vine of the South. I tilted my head backward, under the back window. Facing up into the sky, I could see stars.

Alabama, like some other parts of the Deep South, retains a feeling of the primal American garden. The forests beyond the cotton fields can be primordially rich and inviting and sinister. The South is the home of America's original sin: the enslavement of blacks.

Now, at night, I saw the back of George Junior's head silhouetted by our headlights as they washed across the north Alabama woods. George Junior, "Little George," was talking softly, in those Alabama syllables that have had their edges rounded. He was telling about the first time he spoke before a political audience. He had been seven years old. He had stood on a chair at the microphone at a rural Alabama political rally, and delivered a short, halting, memorized speech that said: Dad should be governor again, you all please help. He could not remember the speech exactly.

Little George had his father's eyebrows, a fierce, dense growth bristling out of the forehead, a fighter's truculent eyebrows. But he also had his mother Lurleen's eyes. The father Wallace's eyes were a deep molten brown with ignitions of violence in them. America remembered those ignitions. Wallace had been a sort of incendiary of the right wing. Wallace expressed the almost pagan defiance of the southern Scotch-Irish, a defiance that was racist, but not only that. It was also hotly antigovernment—one of the oldest American strains. Wallace had risen out of tribal America, touchy and estranged and quick to take offense and to punish.

The tragedy of the South was that the honor of the white tribe came to depend upon the subservience of the black. Wallace cried, "Segregation now! Segregation forever!" He built his career upon a snarling racial politics. He once lost a political race to a man more ostentatiously bigoted than he, and he vowed, "I'll never be out-niggered again!"

Little George sat in the Cadillac and described how as a child during the 1968 presidential primary campaign in Michigan, "I watched while my father just set a crowd on fire. Set them on fire!"

"Was that frightening?" I asked.

A pause. "Yes."

Anyway, Wallace led a Pickett's Charge across a vast suburban parking lot, Middle America, and ended in a tragic mess, shot six times by a rooming-house psychotic, and then installed in a wheelchair for the rest of his life.

Little George's mother, the late Lurleen Wallace, who once served as governor of Alabama when her husband was ineligible to succeed himself in office, had somewhat stricken and compassionate eyes, as I remembered them, and I thought that her son had inherited her gifts of sympathy. He was not, like his father, bristling and bruised. He had not his father's cunning or rage. Little George wore glasses. He spoke with a likable mildness and decency and intelligence.

Here, I thought, that night as we drove down from Scottsboro, was another of the surprising American transformations. America is filled with these stories. The essence of America is the process of change, the possibility of change — change that is sometimes violent, and sometimes filled with a strange and lovely grace.

It is worth thinking about the Wallace trajectory: old genes filtered through new genes, the old South proceeding into the new South, the most defiant American past making friends with the future. The son modifies the father, the present transforms the past, a place becomes different: America becomes different. That transforming energy is the best thing about America. But it is also a form of obliviousness. America is forgetful of the past. It is sometimes difficult for outsiders to understand that that forgetfulness is often the secret of American success.

The South is the one place where the past is supposed to mean something. We were riding south that night from Scottsboro, the home of the Scottsboro Boys, nine blacks accused in 1931 of raping a white girl. They were actors in one of the primal cases of the American racial tragedy. The Scottsboro Boys were the Sacco and Vanzetti of the South. And we were headed for Montgomery, the capital of the old Confederacy. In 1861, from the balcony of the state capitol there, Jefferson Davis, the president of the Confederacy, took his oath of office. His enterprise was to destroy the United States. From that same balcony, I could see the Dexter Avenue Baptist church where Martin Luther King, Jr., ran his long civil-rights campaign against George Wallace.

George Junior was close to his father. A few nights before his father was shot in Maryland, George Junior had a dream in which just such a shooting occurred, except that in the dream, his father died.

George Junior was working now as the director of student finance at Troy State University. He said that every day at the breakfast table he would tell his father stories, true stories about black people's troubles raising money for education. George Junior said that his father sometimes wept in sympathy while he listened.

I drove one September afternoon to a park at Noccalula Falls, near

Gadsden, Alabama, where Governor Wallace was to speak to a labor rally and picnic. Given the history of racial hatred in Alabama, what astonished me was a tenderness. An odd, sweet light came upon the field and grove. After their rally the people rested almost dreamily on the threadbare grass. George Wallace sat in his wheelchair on the small flatbed metal stage. The people came to him. They fell into a long orderly line to file past, take his hand and have him sign their Wallace posters.

Their faces mixed awe, deep familiarity and shyness. They were blue-collar people and farmers who worked the hills of North Alabama. Mostly they had rough country faces and washed, flat, distantly Celtic eyes, eyes like white-blue cracked ice.

There were blacks in the crowd, too. Some of Wallace's campaign workers were black, and in the election that year many of the state's blacks voted for him. They said he was a populist who would help the state attract jobs they badly needed. He had appeared before the assembled blacks at the Southern Christian Leadership Conference in Birmingham that summer and apologized for his old segregationist politics. Black civil-rights leaders who fought Wallace for years were incredulous.

"Have you changed in your attitude toward blacks?" I asked George Wallace late one night. He had telephoned me at my hotel in Montgomery after I had persuaded his son George to intercede. His voice, talking to a man from the northern press, which he despised, had a slurred darkness and warning in it. But when he heard this question, his voice changed register a little. "No," he said, "I have respected and loved them always." What was one to make of that? I was in the presence of stupendous fraud or else miraculous transformation.

At the labor rally in Gadsden, people in wheelchairs were pushed up to his wheelchair, and George Wallace reached out gentle communing hands to them and spent long moments with each, consoling and almost, one thought, healing. Wallace had the nimbus of saint and martyr—or, at any rate, of a celebrity who had passed through the fire and the greater world; he had come back to them from history, come back with powder burns.

Other trajectories: When I was a child in Washington, D.C., during the 1950s, Robert Kennedy played touch football on a playground field in Georgetown not far from the house where my family lived. Kennedy worked then for Senator Joseph McCarthy's investigating committee. Kennedy was thin and tough and boyish. He wore loose khaki Bermuda shorts and a crewneck sweater with an Oxford cloth button-down shirt under it—the shirttail always hanging out the back from under the sweater. Kennedy brought his wife, Ethel, along, and a few children and an enormous Newfoundland dog.

It was a pickup game and I sometimes joined in. We played Kennedy football—meaning that one could pass from anywhere on the field, not merely from behind the line of scrimmage. It was touch football with no tackling allowed, but it was a fairly rough version. Elbows and shoulders flew. People got knocked over and skinned a little. Ethel was almost always pregnant, but she played anyway, the game being coeducational, and Bobby Kennedy would yell at her when she dropped a pass. He cared about winning the game, and it made him mad when Ethel loused up.

Byron White, now a justice of the U.S. Supreme Court, came to the Sunday games sometimes. He had been an all-American football player in college—Whizzer White. He threw perfect long-bomb passes, standing on his own goal line, dodging lightly as the Georgetown gentry came barreling in across the line. White would wait until his receivers were far downfield, and then let fly a perfect spiral that bored through the air in an arc, and then arrived exactly in the receiver's fingers.

One day I was playing on White's side, with Kennedy on the other team. In the huddle, White told me to run long, down the right sideline. I did so, with Bobby Kennedy in hot pursuit. I ran the length of the field, a step in front of Kennedy, and stretched out my arms, scarcely looking back. The ball dropped into my hands, and I was across the goal line. Kennedy gave me a grin.

The Kennedys' experience in America has been a fascinating model of American trajectories and, of course, of the dangers that attend the transformations.

John Kennedy seemed in some ways the perfect American. As the historian Doris Kearns has pointed out, Jack Kennedy exemplified two usually contradictory strains in American tradition. One was the immigrant experience, the old American story of the luckless or disfavored or dispossessed who came from Europe and struggled in the New World. Rooted in that experience was the glorification of the common man and the desire for a common-man presidency, a celebration of the ordinary. The other strain was the American longing for an aristocracy, the buried dynastic, monarchical urge. "Jack is the first Irish Brahmin," said Paul Dever, a former Massachusetts governor. Kennedy had both Harvard and Honey Fitz in him. He was an intellectual who could devastate any woman in the room, devour David Cecil's *Life of Melbourne* in a speedreader's blitz and curse like the sailor he also was.

After Jack's death, Bobby Kennedy began a process of deep change. The histrionics of the sixties, the assassinations and riots, the Vietnam war, all worked transformations in his politics and his character. It seemed to me a deeply moving and very American process — Kennedy suffering through the country's changes, and changing himself.

But then his trajectory, like his brother's, was ended in mid flight.

The news from the California primary was still on the television. I lay in bed and dozed. I woke when I heard the shots and shouting. Bobby Kennedy lay on the floor of the hotel kitchen.

The moon over Los Angeles, the western edge of the American dream.

Previous pages: *Plumes of steam explode in a sulphurous glow at Jupiter Terrace, Yellowstone Park. This national park is famous for its geysers, hot springs and steam vents. The unusually hot rocks below the surface turn water to steam.*

Left: *The hustle and bustle of the Stock Exchange in New York City, financial heart of the United States.*

Right: *The stainless-steel Art Deco spire of the Chrysler Building. It was built in 1929, when at 77 stories it was the tallest building in the world—a record it held until the Empire State Building was built a few months later.*

Right: *The bronze statue of Prometheus watches the Christmas skaters at the Rockefeller Center in New York City. This building complex combines elegance with functionalism. Built in the 1930s, the center remains a place where people can enjoy themselves, whether they prefer the famous murals and sculptures or the ice skating rink.*

Left: *Listening to the music of the spheres: Radio telescope receivers like these have helped make New Mexico a center for space and nuclear research.*

Below: *Moving on the fast track in Atlanta: a modern mass transit system and a period of industrial expansion and construction growth have made Atlanta one of the country's fastest growing urban areas.*

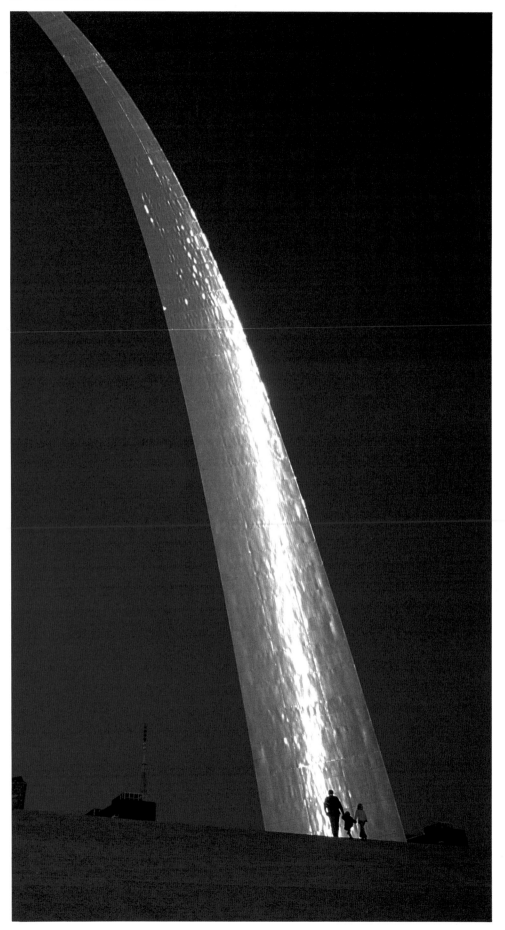

Previous pages: *A bicyclist against the extraterrestrial geometries of Dallas.*

Above: *Cars hurry across the Golden Gate Bridge. Built in the 1930s to connect San Francisco to northern California, it is one of the world's longest suspension bridges.*

Left: *The Gateway Arch in St. Louis, Missouri, on the banks of the Mississippi River. It was designed as the golden parabola of the American dream. It also looks, less impressively, something like one half of the logo of McDonald's hamburger chain.*

Right: *Mardi Gras in New Orleans is famous for its spectacular costumes. The carnival begins on Twelfth Night, January 6, and climaxes on Shrove Tuesday, the day before Lent begins.*

Left: *A beacon to all: Hollywood, dream capital of the world.*

Below: *It is a 700-foot plunge down the Hoover Dam, one of the highest concrete dams in the world. So named because it was started during Herbert Hoover's administration, the dam blocks the Colorado River forming Lake Mead, a reservoir.*

The green argon tubes outlining Dallas's Interfirst Plaza glow eerily against the night sky.

Previous pages: *People have used lighthouses as long as they have sailed the open seas. Storm-driven sailors searched anxiously for their lights to warn of rocks and reefs and to signal that home was near.*

Above: *The spectacular size of this flamingo sign in South Carolina gives it a grandeur that is peculiarly American.*

Left: *Its head high above the clouds, the 110-story Sears Tower in Chicago is a monument to merchandising and architecture. Sears, Roebuck and Company, as whose headquarters the building serves, is one of the world's largest retail stores.*

Ten percent of the population of San Diego was born in Mexico, a fact colorfully reflected in this mural in Chicano Park. Mexican Americans— or Chicanos, as they call themselves—played an important part in U.S. history.

Left: *For those to whom shopping is a way of life, Macy's department store in New York with its 2,151,000 square feet of floor space is heaven on earth.*

Right: *"Sheer Insanity"—a window display in Houston, Texas, and a sign of the times.*

Above: *Tourists in a swirl of lights at the EPCOT Center at Walt Disney World in Orlando, Florida.*

Previous pages: *Lift-off! The launch of the Space Shuttle at Kennedy Space Center in Florida. From this site the United States launched its first satellite in 1958, its first manned space flights in 1961, and its first manned spaceship to the moon in 1969.*

Above: *An island of rural simplicity: an Amish farm. The Amish, who belong to a denomination of the Mennonite church, refuse modern technological advances.*

Left: *The confluence of urban energy: Fifth Avenue in New York City.*

TO
ONE
GORDON
Champ
BEST MUSICAL
FOR SPEC
ELEGANC
ONE
MINUTE
A MONTH
Nationa
BEYOND the DOOR
THE
EXOR

Previous pages: *Times Square, New York—with its lights, theaters, tourists, traffic, noise, pornography, and edge of violence.*

Right: *Wall Street in New York has become synonymous with banking and business. Where now workers toil in skyscrapers there was once a timber wall built by the Dutch in the seventeenth century for protection against attack. The English dismantled the wall in 1699 but the name remains.*

Left: *America is a nation on wheels. Traffic in New York enters and leaves the city by bridges and tunnels.*

Below: *The Lax Theme Building at Los Angeles International Airport hangs like a spaceship caught in midflight.*

remarked that their innocence makes Americans the most dangerous people in the world.

American innocence exists more in the American imagination than in reality. D.H. Lawrence went to the other extreme. He urged his readers to "look through the surfaces of American art, and see the inner diabolism. . . . The essential American soul," Lawrence wrote extravagantly, "is hard, isolate, stoic and a killer." In nineteenth-century portrayals, Uncle Sam had a certain look in his eye that disappeared by the time of the famous First World War I WANT YOU recruiting poster. The old look was conniving, raw and whip-mean, the squint-shrewd eye of a man with a rope who is a week's ride from the nearest law court.

The generation of the sixties came upon this side of the American character with an air of shocked discovery, with the sudden rage of people who felt they had been lied to by the myth. The American history they had been taught did not show them the violent underside of their huge and diverse nation, and they therefore fell headlong into an apocalyptic absolutism common among Americans. If they are not the best in the world, then, they imagine, they must be the worst. The psychological pattern still applies. The triumphal Reaganism of the first six years of the eighties — "Morning in America" — was the almost inevitable response to the sixties and seventies.

The barrels roll from one side of the ship to the other, and presently they roll back again. The vessel plunges on.

There is a moment in one of Vladimir Nabokov's Berlin novels when the narrator sees a mirror being unloaded from a van. Suddenly, the mirror, by a tilt of grace, becomes "a parallelogram of sky."

A sentence of Ralph Waldo Emerson's is sometimes like that: the mind held at an unexpected angle . . . a sudden burst of lovely blue light. It is not a transcendental illumination, exactly. Transcendentalism was a short-lived American moonshine. Emerson's light is brighter. It glows with an eerily sweet intelligence and morning energy. Emerson's sentences make a moral flute music — prose as a form of awakening. They move in a dance of sensual abstractions, small miracles of rhetoric. He had no genius for massive literary architecture. He dealt in the lustrous fragments of his essays, in a succession of quiet flashes.

Anyone who wishes to understand the United States should read Emerson. It is strange that this orphic saint who dined on clouds should have become the prophet of the American civilization's strenuous materialism. He was America's first international-class man of letters. He gave America a metaphysics. He sought to join the nation's intellect to its power. Emerson sanctified America's ambitions. Like the nation, he was, he said, "an endless seeker, with no past at his back." He was America's bishop, the mystic of its possibilities.

For a mild ex-Unitarian clairvoyant dead more than a hundred years, Emerson still stirs surprising controversy. In a baccalaureate address to his senior class, the former president of Yale University, A. Bartlett Giamatti, blamed Emerson for the ugliest tendency in the American character — "a worship of power." Emerson, he said, "freed our politics and our politicians from any sense of restraint by extolling self-generated, unaffiliated power as the best foot to place in the small of the back of the man in front of you."

Giamatti was speaking of the Emerson who inspired the entrepreneurial style of self-reliance and blithe rapacity so often mocked by critics of American business. Earlier readers had a deeper problem with Emerson. His voice seemed too rarefied — ethereal to the point of disconnection with reality — and demonstrably incomplete. He seemed almost bizarrely and wilfully ignorant about the darker side of things. The novelist Henry James put his finger on Emerson's weakness with an exquisite condescension: a "ripe unconsciousness of evil . . . is one of the most beautiful signs by which we know him." The Candide of Concord, Massachusetts.

Emerson is not read nearly enough anymore. He was the rhapsodist of beginnings. He cut loose from the granite Thou Shalt Nots of his forebears, seven generations of New England clergy. The late twentieth century's fantasies tend to focus on endings. Our thoughts seem to flow downward — following a line from Auschwitz and Hiroshima through Cambodia and Bangladesh and Ethiopia. The twentieth century has rarely felt transcendental.

Still, as the philosopher William James explained, "Emerson could perceive the full squalor of the individual fact, but he could see the transfiguration." Emerson had wonderful lines about the fallen world: "It seems as if heaven had sent its insane angels into our world as to an asylum, and here they will break out in their native music and utter at intervals the words they have heard in heaven; then the mad fit returns and they mope and wallow like dogs."

Perhaps the twentieth century is merely one of the moping-dog phases. It may be the sin of pride to claim so much evil and despair for oneself. The Black Death killed off one-third of the population of western and central Europe in the fourteenth century, but in the Emersonian calendar of the perfectible universe, it was only a temporary setback.

Emerson sought to organize the individual soul, not an entire society. He preached the holiness of the conscious mind. That, in part, is what made him so American. America is not a state of being, but becoming.

But America is not so rarefied. It does not float onward through time on a bright crystal of Emersonian becoming. The American business of becoming is an often dangerous and brutal transaction.

The American myth comes equipped with a system of spiritual filters. Americans seem at each moment to view the heroic past in a certain golden nimbus; as the present recedes into the past it seems to acquire a vague glow. The violence is forgotten.

For all of the whooping energy of ambition and greed that Americans showed for so much of their history, there runs through almost every era a deep strain of pessimism, division and violence. George Washington, a marble, Jovian figure in American myth, was attacked all through his presidency as brutally as Richard Nixon ever was. Washington predicted that the thirteen original states would fly apart in civil war and economic chaos. The Federalist Fischer Ames wrote in 1803: "Our country is too big for union, too sordid for patriotism, too democratic for liberty. . . . A democracy cannot last." With President Andrew Jackson bringing the western hordes into American politics in 1835, *Niles' Register* declared: "The state of society is awful. Brute force has superseded the law. . . . The time predicted seems rapidly approaching when the mob shall rule." In fact, lynch mobs, cholera and riots were tearing through the Republic.

Even Walt Whitman, the exuberant poet of the American inclusion, gave way to pessimism in the years after the Civil War. "The problem of the future of America," he wrote in 1871, "is in certain respects as dark as it is vast."

With the arrival of the Great Depression, the critic Edmund Wilson reported matter-of-factly: "The money-making phase of the Republic is over." In the middle of the Eisenhower years, the columnist Murray Kempton wrote: "It is already very hard to remember that, only a generation ago, there were a number of Americans, of significant character and talent, who believed that our society was not merely doomed but undeserving of survival, and to whom every one of its institutions seemed not just unworthy of preservation but crying out to be exterminated."

Americans forget these darker moments. They ignore, too, at least officially, the American strains of isolation, failure, vulnerability and heartbreaking distances. Risk and individualism have always conspired to pitch a lot of Americans out into a freezing, deadly loneliness. Jim Marshall, the first man to discover gold in the California rush, died broke and crazy. Even Thomas Jefferson died in relative penury. Marlboro County, his home in Virginia, was long since depleted.

The triumphal and depressive sides of American life were weirdly combined in President Ulysses S. Grant. He was the obscure American failure who, as commander of the Union forces in the Civil War, saved the Union. His friend General William Tecumseh Sherman, the incendiary of Atlanta, believed that Grant was the typical American, but Sherman also admitted: "I do not understand him, and I do not believe that he understands himself." In political scientist Hannah Arendt's phrase, Adolf Eichmann represented "the banality of evil." In a way, Grant represented the banality of momentary American greatness. Or perhaps the mysterious possibilities of the American ordinary.

Down the generations, Grant has stayed cocooned, in memory, in a stoical mediocrity. The author H.L. Mencken said Grant was the kind of man who would say to someone he encountered: "Meet the wife." He possessed an eerie philistine equilibrium, remarking once that Venice would be a fine city if it were drained. What stuck mostly in memory as the decades passed were the shabby things: the scandals and swindles of his administration and, ignominiously, the talk about his drinking. He did drink too much now and then, when he was depressed and especially when he was away from the stabilizing influence of his wife, Julia, whom he adored.

He had a bewildering but somehow representative American life. What puzzles is his sudden greatness — his rising to the occasion — and the brutality of his greatness, what might be called the bloody abstraction of it. It was as if Grant had rescinded some logic of cause and effect.

In the years before the Civil War, Grant sank into scruffy failure. Men would cross the street when they saw him, fearing that he would try to borrow money from them. He sold cordwood in the streets of Galena, Illinois, to support his family.

Then came the war, and Lincoln's best generals failed. They were theoretically great fighters, but they would not fight. Grant, the failure, succeeded. Down the years, anyone who has bothered to think about Grant has had to wonder whether the man was a genius or a nonentity who blundered into momentary success, who arrived at immortality by accident.

As his death approached, Grant wrote to his physician a note, which contained a subtle and accurate conceit: "The fact is that I think I am a verb instead of a personal pronoun. A verb is anything that signifies to be, to do; or to suffer. I signify all three." It was a perfectly American thought. America thinks of itself as a verb, not a noun, as a nation that does, that acts, not as one that simply is. D.H. Lawrence, in an exercise of comparative spiritual geography, once said that Asia is the place to meditate and Europe is the place to feel; America is the place to act.

It was only as a verb, that is, as a warrior, that Ulysses Grant found focus. Grant had an animal sense of moment and motion. Mary Lincoln, wife of Abraham Lincoln, thought for a time during the siege of Richmond that Grant was a mere "butcher," and most of the North agreed. He was the first genius of industrial warfare.

If there is something haunting about Grant's life, it is the way that, having achieved military greatness and two terms in the White House, he lapsed toward failure again. He became a parable of the unreliability of

American dreams. The American trajectory was supposed to be always ascendant. Grant swooped down, and up, and down again.

And then, at the last, when he was painfully dying of cancer, Grant sat on the front porch of a cottage in the foothills of the Adirondack Mountains in the summer of 1885, and wrote his memoirs, a work of enduring American literature, a parting labor of memory and language from the man of pure action. Grant's labor there in the Adirondacks was a kind of archetype of American retrospection: recollection performed as heroic deed. Improbably Grant became the greatest of the rememberers of a war so morally and dramatically fascinating that Americans have returned to it ever since, generation after generation, as if to a text of inexhaustible meaning.

The Civil War was fought to expunge the American original sin (slavery) and to save the dream and the power. It was all of Homer and Shakespeare come to the New World. It was the American discovery of tragedy and of modern death, proceeding from the jaunty, clumsy toy soldiering of First Bull Run to Sherman's scorched earth and Grant's trench warfare, which were a moral preview of the twentieth century.

The Romanian scholar Mircea Eliade made a distinction between a people's "profane time" and its "sacred time." In sacred time, he thought, deeds partake of the permanence of myth. In his dying hours in the Adirondacks, Grant labored to transport the Civil War, and himself, into sacred time. The war arrived there intact. Grant, however, has remained in a dusk somewhere between myth and Galena, Illinois.

Americans are famously lucky — lucky in their immense natural wealth and vast spaces, in their extraordinary freedom from the stultifications of caste and poverty. The nation seemed born in luck. So at least it seemed to the white Europeans who settled the continent. The Indians they violently displaced and the Africans they brought in chains had a different perspective.

Americans eventually made the mistake of describing their national luck as Manifest Destiny. America became the place where the world came to get lucky. Americans believed in the transforming powers of luck in their land. Men born in poverty made fortunes. They struck oil and gold. Hard work went into it, of course, but for a long time Americans were drunk on the sheer luck of their possibilities.

Generally, luck is something that happens to individuals. If a society or century is considered as a whole, the random events that are set down to luck or fortune form more coherent overall patterns: large historical forces become discernible. But entire societies should not mock luck either. The classic Mayan society disappeared so strangely, so precipitously, that some massive stroke of bad luck must have been at work — a sudden plague, perhaps, or a viral riot.

The satirically pious story tells of a soldier's breast-pocket Bible that stopped the bullet en route to his heart. Ronald Reagan had no Bible in his jacket the day in 1981 John Hinckley, Jr., fired a bullet into him. But his lifelong luck, up to that point, held for him: if the gunman's arm had been jostled by a fraction of an inch, if the angle of the slug's deflection off the president's seventh rib had been minutely sharper, if the Devastator bullet had not been a dud. . . . Of course, one can argue it the other way: if the assassin's arm had been jostled, he might have missed Reagan entirely.

John and Bobby Kennedy had no such luck, nor did Martin Luther King, Jr.

America, with its mobility and relative rootlessness, has always been a pageant of the fortuitous. But luck needs to be tended. A commissioner of baseball, Branch Rickey, defined luck as "the residue of design." There can be no "design" for winning the New York State Lottery, other than buying the tickets. In other areas, it is to some extent true that people make their own luck: given a lucky break, they exploit it.

On the other hand, America can be a cruel place for the luckless. I once spent a couple of winter months traveling around the United States talking to homeless people in public parks, shelters and tent cities. There is a sharp moral dissonance in the spectacle of these men and women living amid wealth — a familiar American violence of effects.

A black woman slept that winter in a large cardboard box beside a wall at the edge of Central Park in New York. Her box, originally used to ship a refrigerator, was just across Fifth Avenue from Jacqueline Onassis's apartment building. I passed the woman every day as I rode my bicycle to midtown. She was well dressed and never looked dirty. She owned a red suit, which she folded neatly when she wasn't wearing it. I kept track of her for several months, checking her every day. I thought to offer her money, but she seemed self-sufficient. I never spoke to her. Then one morning I rode by to find that she was gone.

Traveling among the homeless was a complex experience. The farther I went and the more I talked to them, the more difficult I found it, curiously, to judge what had happened to them. They stirred great sympathy. They also, sometimes, made me very angry, and not at the system that had put them on the streets. I became angry at them, angry at their capitulation, angry at them for being victims. That, of course, was my problem and not theirs.

In Phoenix, I found a Mexican-American family — mother, father, four children — living in a ramshackle trailer. They were thus not technically homeless, but the father could not find work. The mother now and then worked as a maid and brought in a little money, a circumstance that humiliated the father and damaged his pride. He smoldered with a heartbreaking rage at being thus emasculated. His wife showed me a photograph of the entire family, a blurry Kodachrome hanging on the wall of the trailer. It had been mended. Not long before, the husband had ripped the photograph, tearing off the picture of himself; thus violently banishing himself, canceling himself. His wife tenderly Scotch-taped him back into the family again.

I correspond with the family now and then. The father found work in a restaurant. The children are well and going to school. They now have the money to rent a house.

On the other hand, after talking for several hours to a homeless man living with his family in a station wagon beside a park in Long Beach, California, I was filled with contempt for him and for his weakness. He had been an engineer for an aerospace company, and had lost his job, through his own fecklessness, I thought. He was able-bodied and reasonably well-educated but had slipped downward and taken his children down with him. So the whole family lived in the station wagon now, using the public toilets in the park and scouring for handouts.

The man irritated me. I understood later that I was willing to forgive and sympathize with the Mexican, but this engineer was white and middle class — formerly. He stirred obscure anxieties in me.

A young man living in another car in Long Beach, living rather happily, I thought, taught me how to eat well on no money at all. The fast-food restaurants, he said, always ended the day with a surplus of cooked hamburgers, fried chicken, French fries and so on that could not be saved for the next day. The restaurants did not advertise the fact, but if you went around to the back door at closing time, around midnight, there was plenty to eat.

I was not sure that it was a reliable way to stay alive. I found out that anyone on the street for a few days or weeks learns the hours of the soup kitchens, the routines of the shelters. I fell in with a group of homeless men in Chicago, on the edge of the Loop. Their days were as intricately timed and regular as a business executive's. They left their shelter at 6:30 AM, and went to a soup kitchen for coffee and doughnuts. Then they gathered around an empty oil drum in a vacant lot, and built a fire in it. They warmed themselves around the fire through the morning, until another soup kitchen opened for lunch. . . . And so on through the day.

The mission in which they slept was a Dickensian place, brutally Christian and hateful. The people who ran it hated the homeless and thought of them as vermin. On very cold days, the men were penned in a large lobby, at close quarters, and they stood there all day, smoking, talking in low tones, sometimes arguing and threatening each other. The windows steamed with the bitter cold blowing off Lake Michigan. The men in the lobby gave off the overpowering sour smell of bathlessness and homelessness and anxiety and defeat.

America can be heartless and squalid if one is out of money and luck, and living on the streets, sleeping on the heating grates. On the other hand, America is the salvation and a new chance at life to millions of new immigrants every year, including those who sneak across the Mexican border at night or float up in small boats from Haiti.

It was once a sort of religious obligation, like the Muslim hajj, for European journalists, novelists, poets and hacks to make their way to the New World and there to test their sensibilities upon the vast savage novelty of America. For years in the nineteenth century, visiting writers could not decide whether the Americans were a vigorous new race, "a new order of man," as Henry Adams said, or something less. Earlier, Samuel Johnson, irritated by their revolution, called them "a race of convicts."

English writers arrived in the United States the way an ex-wife might visit the home of a remarried husband some years after a messy divorce.

The ex-wife, dressed to kill, encases her curiosity in a ladylike frost. She notices things brutally, and repeats them when she gets home.

Mrs. Frances Trollope reported back to England in 1832 that Americans gorge their food with "voracious rapidity." They swill, guzzle, spit and pick their teeth with pocketknives. In Cincinnati, she related, cows are nonchalantly milked at the house door, and pigs wander at will, rooting in the street garbage and nuzzling pedestrians with their snouts.

Charles Dickens reported back that Americans have no sense of humor. Oscar Wilde descended in an overcoat of bottle-green otter fur. He lectured the miners in Leadville, Colorado, on the Florentine painters. He hired secretaries to distribute locks of his hair.

Foreign interpreters arrived like immigrant waves, and each found a different America. Interpreters have thought that America was primitive, hostile, desolate, vacant, dazing, Edenic, blessed, obstreperous, eagle-screaming, slave-driving, egalitarian, myth-stained, rapacious, naive, extroverted, hospitable, dangerous, destined, sanctimonious, shrewd, sentimental, quick, profligate, protean, complacent, oblivious, uncultured, venal, generous, banal, violent, abstracted, insecure, guilt-stricken, self-lacerating, tolerant and ultimately indefinable.

I suppose all the words applied, and some still do. Soviet journalists who visit like to add adjectives like drug-crazed, crime-ridden, homeless, pitiless and capitalist.

Cincinnati has certainly improved since Mrs. Trollope was nuzzled by the pigs.

*In the glow of an orange sunset, a canoe
glides through the Florida Everglades.*

Previous pages: *The towers of the Golden Gate Bridge rise above one of the magic cotton fogs that nestle into San Francisco Bay.*

Left: *The Washington Monument, a great obelisk built to honor George Washington, is visited by one million people a year. Washington was not only the first president, he also commanded the Continental Army that won American independence and served as president of the convention that wrote the Constitution.*

Above: *"Proclaim Liberty throughout all the land unto all inhabitants thereof," reads the inscription on the Liberty Bell, rung on July 8, 1776, to announce the adoption of the Declaration of Independence. It is no longer rung but hangs in a pavilion north of Independence Hall in Philadelphia.*

Right: *"Four score and seven years ago our fathers brought forth on this continent a new nation, conceived in liberty and dedicated to the proposition that all men are created equal." To preserve that nation, Abraham Lincoln led the United States through a Civil War. The Lincoln Memorial in Washington, D.C., commemorates his contribution.*

Left: *The Jefferson Memorial in Washington, D.C., a circular, white marble building, was completed in 1943, on the 200th anniversary of Jefferson's birth. The design is based on the classical style of architecture which Jefferson introduced to the United States.*

Previous pages: *Many of America's once glorious cities have deteriorated into slums and urban wastelands. As people moved away from the city's core, they took with them the hope and vitality that had once fueled it.*

Below: *In many small towns the church serves as both a spiritual and social center—the unifying force of the community.*

Above: *In addition to his skills as a politician, Thomas Jefferson was a gifted inventor and architect. He built Montecello in Virginia in 1776, and although he was publicly opposed to slavery, he kept over 100 slaves there.*

Right: *The only court created specifically by the Constitution, the Supreme Court in Washington is the highest in the land and helps guarantee equal justice to all Americans.*

SYMBOLS

I like to collect resonant American malapropisms. The author Walker Percy told of a Mississippi black man who identified a certain bird as the "blue dollar hawk." It turned out later that the bird was correctly called the "blue darter hawk." Here, as Mark Twain said, is the difference between lightning and lightning bug. The blue dollar hawk has a splendidly enigmatic name. It represents both buried history (somewhere in the lore there is a reason it was called that—why dollar, and why blue?) and a poetic transfiguration: the idea of money given feathers and flight. It is a name that sends out a mysterious vibration for an instant, a pleasing flash and blur of extra meanings. The blue darter hawk, on the other hand, describes itself in a drearily literal-minded way. It is about as mysterious as a Chevrolet.

The novelist John Irving imagined a child at the beach who looked out and darkly warned about the "undertoad," a monster lurking out where the waves broke, ready to bear him out to sea. Beware of the undertoad.

The summer my son James was four years old, I took him to Yankee Stadium sometimes to watch the New York Yankees play baseball. James wore a miniature Yankees uniform with the number of his hero, Reggie Jackson, number forty-four. At the start of each game, of course, the national anthem was played, boomingly. James had the impression that it was called "The Star Spangled Banger," and always referred to it thus.

Exactly. "Star-Spangled Banger" perfectly catches both the song and the flag itself. The anthem is almost always rendered as a kind of banger, even when it is played at baseball stadiums on the organ, an instrument that somehow resists playing the song.

"The Star-Spangled Banner" is an ungainly anthem, with a thumping insistence in the music that ends in unsingable high reaches. Its lyrics are grammatically bizarre, a strange carpentry of dangling clauses tacked on with dogged illogic (". . . at the twilight's last gleaming, whose broad stripes and bright stars . . ."). They are filled with bomb bursts and glares, an eruption of inexplicable violent fireworks.

"The Star Spangled Banner" celebrates an utterly forgotten battle (at Fort McHenry in Baltimore Harbor) in a war (that of 1812) that not one American in five thousand could explain. The anthem begins with the words and music reproducing the sound of heavy oak furniture being moved around a large, gloomy room, and then ("and the rockets' red glare, the bombs bursting in air . . .") ventures outdoors and flaps its wings, and tries to get airborne, but cannot. It labors along and then strains skyward again. After one last screeching attempt ("and the la-and of the freeeeee") it subsides back to earth, collapsing with three hard thuds (". . . of . . . the . . . brave").

It has never seemed to me a very handsome national anthem. It cannot stir, for example, like "La Marseillaise." But perhaps "La Marseillaise" is an exception among the world's national anthems. Most anthems, considered purely as pieces of music detached from their emotional significance, sound bogus and blockheaded. Consider "Deutschland Uber Alles," or "O Canada." The best anthem, I judge, is "Waltzing Matilda."

Of course, a national anthem takes its meaning precisely from its emotional associations, from what it stands for, not what it proclaims. Only two American singers, Ray Charles and Lou Rawls, to my knowledge, have made "The Star Spangled Banner" sound like a good song. But it stirs Americans nonetheless.

The American flag is also a banger. It is bold and even garish, bright primary colors arranged somewhat improbably — one blue quadrant dense with white stars, and the stripes streaming out loosely, expansively. The flag includes but does not integrate two conflicting messages:

an intricate density of stars in the crowded blue patch, and the flowing, uncrowded ease of the other three-quarters of the flag: the stripes. One mustn't be too pedantic with the flag, but it strikes me that the design suggests both the openness of American landscape and, in the field of stars, something crowded and complex and demanding: the cities, perhaps.

In any case, the American flag has occupied a much stronger place in American life and mythology than have flags of other countries. In a nation created as an experiment, a republic as much willed as evolved, the flag has embodied an entire national idea. In "one nation under God," that idea implies divinity. For some Americans, the flag is literally a sacred object. The evangelist Billy Graham once said: "The American flag is what a black man means when he says Soul. It's like the Queen of England — the flag is our queen."

Americans, from the beginning, have needed to cling to their symbols, the idea of their unity. The symbol was needed to reinforce a somewhat tenuous reality — that is, that so many people from so many different places around the world can be made to form a new tribe in a new world and can make it work.

Albert Camus wrote in one of his essays: "We will not win our happiness with symbols. We'll need something more solid." No doubt. However, images and symbols can mobilize or demoralize a nation's will in a sometimes alarming way, and this tends to be especially true among Americans, who constantly question who they are and what they represent.

Ronald Reagan understood this American trait. Both consciously and instinctively he manipulated it in order to recrystallize a national morale that began going sour sometime in the middle sixties and remained troubled — through Vietnam, Watergate, the Arab oil crisis, the Iranian hostage episode — until the economic recovery a couple of years after Reagan came to the White House.

The flag, and patriotism, began to be respectable again in America around the time of the nation's bicentennial celebration in 1976. The year turned into a flag-waving ceremony of self-forgiveness.

In the winter of 1980, the Iranians were holding their American hostages. The president, Jimmy Carter, a man with gifts of leadership to match his Southern diminutive, had pronounced that a "malaise" lay upon America. The malaise, of course, lay upon Jimmy Carter, who sought to generalize his own defects and doze off into a dream of his own blamelessness.

Then, in the Winter Olympics, a team of amateur American hockey players defeated the Soviet team, and the United States erupted in celebration. Huckleberry Finn destroyed Ivan the Terrible. The hockey victory had no material meaning at all. It was merely a hockey game, a symbol. But the very innocence of the conquest (unlike the Soviet invasion of Afghanistan not long before) made it sweetly uncomplicated and morally unimpeachable. And so the United States indulged in small orgies of flag waving and anthem singing. At a Stop & Shop supermarket in Cambridge, Massachusetts, the PA system suddenly announced that the U.S. hockey team had beaten the Soviets, and the store was filled with bags of cookies and paper towels as anything handy was tossed in the air with wild cheering.

There was a time — or there have been times — when an American's feelings about his or her country and flag were fairly simple. But for some years, starting in the sixties, those feelings became painfully complicated. The American mind was overrun by civil war. Symbols, in that war, acquired a power that ultimately exceeded the power of military weapons. It was symbols, images and gestures that ended America's longest war, not bullets, not military hardware.

For much of American history, the flag belonged to those who wrapped themselves in it without irony. Politicians, including Abraham Lincoln, published their campaign messages against a flag backdrop. (No one had a better right than Lincoln, surely, since he rescued what the flag represented: American unity.)

During the Vietnam war, the flag became a powerful image in American street theater, and it was appropriated by both sides in the conflict. America itself became a theater in those days, angry, anarchic, the country at war with itself. The opposing American cultures both brandished the same banner: the Silent Majority and the Woodstock Nation each used the flag. The flag became an emblem of American disunity. The antiwar people set the flag on fire. They blew their noses in it, and slept in it and used it to patch the seats of their trousers. Construction workers flew the flag — they still do — from their building sites, and waved it with a defensive pride. Once, only wars abroad prompted Americans to bring out their flags so aggressively. Now it was a war at home.

Or perhaps it was a carnival as well. "Desecrating the flag is just fun," a Berkeley student said in 1970. "It's burned, torn, or worn for the sheer joy of doing something naughty and getting away with it."

Vietnam. Vietnam.

Every American beyond a certain age is a veteran of Vietnam. I think that it is not possible to understand the United States without knowing what Vietnam did to America. It is true that Americans have a short historical attention span, and that the American forgetfulness is sometimes a gift of grace, a protection against obsession. Forgetfulness is a way of getting on with things. Still, I was astonished when I talked to a young woman who did not know what the Tet Offensive was. She was intelligent and well-informed. I was interviewing her as a member of an alumni committee screening candidates for Harvard.

What should we remember? What should we forget? What remembering is necessary? What forgetting is productive? We have a deep moral obligation to remember Dachau and Auschwitz. But to remember everything is to go mad. Memory in America is an endlessly complex subject. Memory goes against the American's official flow of traffic.

The largest American generation, the children of the baby boom, have the Vietnam war embedded in their souls, as the Depression and the Second World War are embedded in the characters of their parents. The memory of the Depression formed the personalities — the fears, premises, predispositions — of an immense generation. Vietnam did the same thing for another generation.

It is important to understand the symbolic and psychological importance of Vietnam especially because those who lived through the experience, those who fought in the war and those who protested the war, are now assuming power in America. Charles Robb, who commanded a Marine rifle company in 1968 and 1969, became the governor of Virginia. Robb will in time likely be a presidential candidate. Bob Kerrey, a Congressional Medal of Honor winner who lost part of a leg in action as a member of the Seals, a Navy special forces unit, became the governor of Nebraska. No one will comprehend power in America, or the people who wield it, unless they know about the formative influence of the Vietnam war upon that generation.

In his novel *Slaughterhouse-Five*, written about the Second World War, Kurt Vonnegut, Jr., imagined a moment of miraculous healing. Everything in war went backward, like a reversed film: bombs magically recombined themselves and sailed upward into the bellies of the airplanes that had dropped them. The planes flew home backward; there, factory workers and scientists labored to disassemble the steel and explosives and bury them in the earth where they would be forever harmless.

But one never escapes back into innocence except by going crazy — Lear's solution, or Ophelia's. The experience of such a war cannot be rescinded, only absorbed, learned from.

The United States lost the war, although technically, of course, the country was out of it by the time of the final collapse of South Vietnam in the spring of 1975. But the loss itself was not as traumatic (for Americans, anyway) as the way the war was fought, the way it was perceived, and peculiarly hated. The struggle was waged savagely in

Southeast Asia. But it was also fought in America, in American institutions, in the American streets, and above all, in the American conscience, in the American mind. Vietnam illustrates perfectly the thought that America is a republic of the mind. Everything that happens in America is vulnerable to a moral weather that hangs in the air, in the unstable present, above the geography and culture and language and custom that serve to anchor most countries.

The war destroyed many lives, American and Vietnamese. It did other damage, to American faith in government and authority, for one thing. But the trauma had its creative side. The events that shattered the American faith in authority also had a sometimes chaotically liberating force, breaking old molds and freeing the imagination to create new forms, new movements (environmentalism, say, or feminism — or even Federal Express, the overnight nationwide delivery service formed by a former helicopter pilot who modeled the business on techniques he learned in organizing chopper missions in Vietnam).

The war brought with it gusts of wild energy. The war, and the protest against it, shook loose forces in American life and gave them a style and prestige they might not otherwise have had. Politics came dancing with a loony phosphorescence. There was a giddy proximity of death at the time — rock stars like Janis Joplin and Jimi Hendrix went tumbling down from drug overdoses, as if to dramatize the war's theme of meaninglessly, profligately blasted youth.

Vietnam was the deepest moral experience for America since the Civil War. Yet, bizarrely, the thing also had a dimension of gaudy American self-indulgence, the war and the music getting together to create a prototype of the rock video. In both the countercultural sideshow and the councils of power that made war policy, there was a note of manic narcissism, of self-importance, almost of autoeroticism. There was dangerous fun in the air, the sheer buzz of so much power, a life-and-death excitement. But someone should have known better.

Sometimes, in the American context, it is difficult to know whether to judge the Vietnam era in historical terms or in psychiatric terms. One can look at it coolly, from the outside, as geopolitics, weighing the gains and losses and ironies of the war. But then there comes, even to the civilian (we are all veterans of Vietnam), a vivid flashback, and the mind fills with the war again. It comes back and back and back. Charles de Gaulle called Vietnam a "rotten country," and he was right in the psychic as well as the military sense. Rotten certainly for Americans. Vietnam took America's energy and innocence — a dangerous innocence, perhaps — and bent them around so that the muzzle fired in the nation's face.

In a sense, the war in Vietnam dictated American political life for a generation. But for the war, Lyndon Johnson might have served two terms. He might have made his Great Society work or at least work better than it ultimately did. He might have been succeeded by Robert Kennedy. All that is, of course, imponderable. As it was, the war shook the Democratic party for years.

But for Vietnam, Richard Nixon might have survived, for it was Vietnam that induced Watergate. Watergate led to Jimmy Carter ("I will never lie to you"), and Carter's peculiar fecklessness led to Ronald Reagan. That was the true domino effect of Vietnam.

The new mood of America, in its recrystallization during the Reagan years, is out of harmony with most of the countercultural forces that gave the United States a certain nihilistic energy in the sixties. The war and the counterculture could at moments seem part of the same rock and roll, drawing their energy from one dark circuit. Grunts in Vietnam sometimes carried their tape players in firefights and listened to the Grateful Dead, to Sam the Sham and the Pharaohs, to the Rolling Stones.

The war has always been refracted rather strangely in the American mind. As time has moved on, the war has also receded, in a psychological sense. During the seventies, the war seemed much farther away than it does in the eighties. During the seventies, Americans indulged in a remarkable exercise of recoil and denial and amnesia about Vietnam. They did not want to think about it, to hear about it.

Perhaps the most important change in American attitudes toward the war during the eighties has been the public acceptance of those who fought in it. The Vietnam veteran, after a long struggle, has acquired a considerable respect.

The long absorption of the experience of Vietnam illustrates the importance of morale in the American mind. Americans need to feel a sense of their own virtue in the world, and Vietnam confused and shamed them. In the residually romantic view (the American view, until Vietnam), war was an essentially knightly exercise — a man riding out in resplendent armor (B-52s, perhaps, Hueys, the light observation helicopters known as Loaches, all of that brilliant American technology) to rescue the innocent from the wicked. In the original versions of the knightly ideal, the wicked were the enemies of Christ, a role for which the Communists qualified.

But when the knights came to seem monstrous, perpetrators of My Lai, then the entire chivalric logic collapsed, and masculinity itself became a horror — all rage and aggression and reptilian brain. Vietnam, among other things, changed American notions about the virtues of masculinity and femininity. In the sixties, during the great violence of the war, masculine power came to be subtly discredited in many minds as vile and destructive. The heritage of the Enlightenment, the scientific method, progress, the dreamy Jeffersonian clarity of mind that told us all problems could be solved, now seemed drawn into a darker business.

Even masculine hormones became suspect. Femininity was the garden of life, masculinity the landscape of death. Perhaps in a subliminal way, the long hair and beads that protesting men wore in the sixties were intended to detoxify them, to take the curse off their masculinity.

The Vietnam Veterans Memorial in Washington became a central symbol of the veterans' struggle for acceptance in America. The memorial was built not by the government but by contributions, mostly from the veterans themselves. The memorial's design — two long triangular panels of polished black granite, set below ground level, inscribed with the names of all the 58,022 Americans who died in Vietnam — struck many veterans as insulting at the time it was chosen. Tom Carhart, a Vietnam veteran and West Point graduate, called it "a black gash of shame." The novelist James Webb, who had become an assistant secretary of defense, wanted a white memorial, set above ground, with a flag. "A memorial should express more than grief," Webb said. "It should honor the service of those who died."

John Wheeler was one of the chief organizers of the drive to get the memorial built after a veteran named Jan Scruggs conceived the idea. In his book, *Touched with Fire*, Wheeler wrote: "Our memories of the events of the Vietnam era still haunt us. They will shape the politics in our generation. . . . The memory is a predicate — implicit or explicit — of government and press pronouncements on El Salvador, Nicaragua, Afghanistan, Poland, Iran, Lebanon, and certainly Southeast Asia."

One cold day in early spring, Jack Wheeler and I walked across the Mall in Washington to the memorial. A wet snow had just begun to fall. We walked down the declivity toward the apex of the black walls. The walkway declines at precisely the angle of escalation of the war, and as we went deeper and deeper into the names of the dead, we were back in the war again. The force of so many names, the names a long incantation, listed in the order of their deaths, and the specificity of the names, each one individual — the names and the deaths being at least incontestable truths in a war that otherwise was a nightmare of illusions and disillusions — the names seen in the black granite that also reflected the sky and our faces (the sky alive, snow moving, clouds moving, and our faces alive in the black polished stone reflection): all produced a profound effect.

The Vietnam Veterans Memorial is visited by more people every year than any other monument in Washington except the Lincoln Memorial. That is a measure of how profoundly the experience of the Vietnam war still inhabits the American heart. The memorial is a sort of shrine, and to it, millions of Americans bring complexities of emotion that go far beyond grief and remembrance. In an uncanny way, the memorial carries one into the mysteries of life and death.

Even so, even so. I take my five-year-old son Justin to Toys "R" Us, and we seek the "action figures." There, arrayed in aisle after aisle, an American Golconda, are thousands of triumphant little Americans with bulging muscles and lethal weapons and righteous homicide in their eyes: G.I. Joe figures, Rambo figures, Captain America.

During the Vietnam war, and through most of the seventies, the conscientious liberal American parent would have no toy guns in the house, no uniforms, none of the militaristic paraphernalia. By the mid-eighties, the children were blasting away at each other again.

As a child in the aftermath of the Second World War, I fired off millions of imaginary rounds of ammunition at my brother, at other children. Guns were wonderful, efficacious things. Our fathers had taken them to Europe and the Pacific and defeated evil with guns. The hardware was magic, brilliant. A line of fatal effect shot from one's brain through the trigger finger — bang! — through the air, and the enemy dropped.

I still like guns, like the smooth heavy weight and precise machining of a good rifle. I still like to shoot, although I have never killed anything other than a dozen doves that I brought down in west Texas one evening.

I doubt that playing with guns turns children into martial maniacs. On the other hand, if I were an Englishman or an Italian, I might behold Americans in the full panoply of their bristling armaments—toy arms and real arms — and grow alarmed at the spectacle. Anyone who has ever been around guns knows that there is something peculiarly seductive about them. The poor children whom America sent to fight in Vietnam (average age: nineteen) were, many of them, seduced by a certain brilliance of weaponry, all the expensive toys the American technology could produce.

One day I flew down to Washington to attend a seminar that Jack Wheeler organized to discuss the Vietnam generation and its future. One of the participants was William Broyles, the former editor of *Texas Monthly* and *Newsweek*. One by one around the table, we introduced ourselves and described what we had done during the war. (I had been a writer at *Time*.) Broyles gave the shortest introduction of any of us. He said he had been in Vietnam, and he was still trying to figure it out. Then he fell silent.

Later, as we all talked, Broyles described a recent reunion that he had had with his comrades from the war.

"For the first day and a half," said Broyles, "we talked about how awful the war was. But there came a time when we stopped that, and we looked at each other . . . and we admitted that it had been . . . *fun!*" Broyles uttered the last word with a complex look mixing self-knowledge, fierce pagan glee, and rue.

Later, Broyles went back to Vietnam and found the field where he had fought, and even found the enemy he had fought, and he came to a complicated peace with Vietnam.

Gloria Emerson covered the war for the *New York Times* from 1970 to 1972. She wrote about it then, and afterward, with a fierce intelligence and indignation. In the mid-seventies I had lunch with her in New York City. I said something about the traumatic effects of Vietnam upon the United States, and Gloria demurred. "The country was not particularly shattered by the war," she said. "We are an inattentive and self-absorbed people. I suppose that inattention is also a protection of sorts. We are a people who drop the past and then forget where it has been put."

Later that afternoon, we found Ward Just, a novelist and reporter who covered the war for the *Washington Post*. We went to an Irish bar on Third Avenue and talked about the war and how it affected America.

Just said, "The country is divided into two nations where Vietnam is concerned — those deeply touched by what happened there (and they are a minority) and those not affected (a very large majority)."

Perhaps. As the poet Robert Lowell wrote about Americans: "Life by definition must breed on change./ Each season we scrap old cars and wars and women." But that is not entirely right either. America is capable of remarkably complex emotional effects. Healing is not mere forgetfulness.

It is interesting to trace the course of American popular thinking about the war through television shows and movies. During the late seventies, the Vietnam veteran was often portrayed as a murderous psychotic (as in the 1976 movie *Taxi Driver*) or as a drug-maddened, haunted loser. In *Coming Home*, he became more sympathetic, though in one character he was a cripple, and in another, bitter, troubled and suicidal. *The Deer Hunter* ended with an elegiac singing of "God Bless America" in a blue-collar bar in Pennsylvania.

But then in the eighties the story lines changed. The Vietnam veteran became a self-reliant hero, like Tom Selleck in the television series *Magnum P.I.* or the cartoon heroes of *The A-Team*. Soon, self-reliance turned aggressive again. Sylvester Stallone's Rambo eventually returned to Vietnam on a mission to rescue Americans still held there by evil Vietnamese characters who looked like the wily despicable Japanese in Second World War American movies. Popular fantasy reversed the moral onus that Americans had long felt about the war. Americans were the victims now, not the aggressors, and they were therefore justified in exacting brutal revenge, as Rambo did, as Chuck Norris did in a similar movie called *Missing in Action*. In the American imagination, the Vietnam veteran had been given back his manhood, and then some. It was only with *Platoon* that an American filmmaker, Oliver Stone, confronted the ambiguous mess and tragedy of Vietnam.

The Rambo side of America makes the rest of the world edgy — at least if the rest of the world believes that these fantasies of power and revenge, these cartoons of foreign policy, represent the official disposition of American government. Sometimes they do, as in Ronald Reagan's bombing of Tripoli. When the president of the United States uses a line from a Clint Eastwood movie ("Go ahead, make my day"), inviting a felon to get his head blown off, the world stirs uncomfortably.

If there is a peculiarly saving grace about the Vietnam war, it may reside with the seven hundred thousand Indochinese who came to America, like so many immigrants and refugees from around the world, and made new lives for themselves. If they were brought to the United States by tragedy and by the destruction of their pasts, they were also proceeding with the construction of a future. Like all first-generation immigrants, they feared that their children would lose the old culture. They asked questions in Vietnamese, and their children replied in English. In Orange County, California, where ninety thousand Vietnamese settled, the parents ran shops selling jewelry and herbs, ginseng and pickled ginger. They worried about their children wearing punk hairdos and staying out at night. They sent packages of food to their families in Ho Chi Minh City. They thought about the past a lot.

Stars and stripes: a symbol and a
decoration—and a hat.

Previous pages: *The faces of four presidents—George Washington, Thomas Jefferson, Theodore Roosevelt, and Abraham Lincoln —are carved into the cliffs of Mount Rushmore, a 5,600-foot-high mountain in the Black Hills of South Dakota.*

Left: *The bald eagle was chosen as the U.S. national bird in 1782. This bird's fierce and proud appearance and its ability to soar high in the air have made it the ideal symbol of freedom and power.*

Right: *Once numbering in the millions, the American bison is now almost extinct in the wild, killed as the railway and settlers moved west. A skilled marksman was said to be able to kill 150 animals in a day.*

Below: *Looking as romantic as a shady past, white columned mansions like this symbolize Louisiana's past glory as the leader of the Old South.*

HOWARD E BARDEN · DAVID D BERKHOLZ · GARY E BULLOCH
EDWARD P HANSHAW · MICHAEL T JONES · ROY R KUBLEY ·
ORRIS · HARVEY MULHAUSER · ERNEST T DUPONT · WILLIAM H S
ALKER · MERRILL V BEASLEY · WILLIAM A BEYER · JOHN C BOHANN
A Jr · WALTER R DALEY · DAVID J FRISCHMANN · JAMES D HENDER
BERT W MARTIN · JAMES P McGRATH · RICHARD P McSTRAVICK Jr
VILLARD A PHILSON · ROBERT J PRAZINKO · JERRY D WORTHY ·
ELL · WILLIAM D SCHADDELEE · JOHN H WELCH III · LEONARD RC
JOHN A DABONKA · JOE R FULGHUM Jr · ROGER D HERRANDO ·
SON · EDWARD E MANNS · THOMAS M MARTINEZ · LUIS G MOR
THY · MARION G RUNION · LARRY E SMITH · LARRY E SMITH ·
VART · ALAN H ZIMMERMAN · MARCO J BARUZZI · HAROLD E BEF
S · RAYMOND F DEMORY · ADAM FISCHER · JAMES E FORSMAN ·
NSON · PAUL R KARAS · FERNANDO LEAL · HAROLD E LEE ·
R PHILLIPS · STEPHEN C SANGER · PAUL T SHORT Jr · PHILIP J SMIT
· ALVIN G TENNISON · JACKSON THOMAS · ROGER B TJERNBERG
WARE · DAN T WASHINGTON · DAVID W WEHRS · ROBERT L ARM
COLLAMORE Jr · RONALD C KISSINGER · HERB DOBY ROBERT F
STONE · GARY L JONES · WILLIAM D DAUGHERTY · LARRY E LEE ·
MARK · JOSEPH R MARTINEZ · ROBERT W MOYER · SAMUEL D McC
R · ROBERT L SHAFER · CHARLES M SHELTON · EDWA F SMITH ·
RELLI · DONALD E THOMPSON · JOE F WALKER · D IS WILBUR
T F STARBUCK · JAMES C WINSTON · RICHARD A V · CLIFFO
ADY · ULYSSES G BURROUGHS · DAVID D DAVEN LEON N
RD · JAMES R PAUL · HENRY R LOPEZ · MICHAE T R PO
MFORD · JAMES F McELYEA · GERALD LEE LARS MILLE
BERTS · JAMES H SCOTT · IRA J SPITTLER III · J UEL J
ARRINGTON Jr · DONALD R BAIR · MAX E P Y E CRC
SSEY · GEORGE J CARRILLO Jr · GILMORE W SYDNE
M ROBERTS · PATRICK J FORAN · WILLIAM A KIBBEY ·
L · LUCIUS L HEISKELL · FRED A JOHNSON NALD W McNE
MERRHAGE M MOYER · CARLOS N V FLETCHER · KENN
M NOWACK · WILLIAM J ROBBINS · KEN

Left: *The Vietnam Memorial in Washington is inscribed with the names of the approximately 58,000 Americans who died in the Vietnam War. Many veterans thought the memorial should be white, conventional and heroic. But the dark wall has become a kind of shrine, and in its way it is a spiritual masterpiece of grieving and reconciliation.*

Above: *The U.S.S. **Arizona** Memorial honors those who died in a surprise Japanese attack on Pearl Harbor on December 7, 1941. This act opened hostilities between Japan and the United States in the Second World War. The Memorial stands above the partly submerged battleship **Arizona**, where more than a thousand men are entombed.*

The Stars and Stripes, the Star Spangled Banner, Old Glory—whatever it is called, the flag has symbolized the American will in both victory and defeat. Even hanging from a porch on a peaceful summer's day, it evokes a country's heritage in a way that no other nation's flag does.

Left: *Harvard University, the oldest in the United States, has set an intellectual standard for the country and has produced many great thinkers and statesmen, including five presidents.*

Right: *Small-town America, epitomized in the work of Norman Rockwell, symbolizes for many the true values of the people.*

Left: *The flag flies between the Wrigley and Tribune buildings in Chicago.*

Right: *The rodeo turned the old cowboy skills—riding, roping and the rest— into spectacle, a Western version of the circus.*

Below: *A Navajo medicine man surrounded by the symbols of many cultures.*

Previous pages: *Fourth of July celebrations in Vermont—a birthday party to which everyone is invited.*

THE TEXAS MYTH

The cowboy has his place in American myth. But ranchers these days find it hard sometimes to recruit young men for the work, which is tedious and pays poorly.

It was the cold early spring of 1886 in the Dakota Badlands, and Theodore Roosevelt was angry. A man called Redhead Finnegan and a couple of other drifters had stolen Roosevelt's rowboat and taken off down the Little Missouri River. With two friends, Roosevelt went after the thieves.

Roosevelt and his men rode a scow downriver for three days, pushing through the ice jams. They came upon the thieves' camp and captured them without a fight. A practical man would have obeyed the custom of the territory and hanged the three right there. Some Dakotans were mystified by the course Roosevelt chose. He struggled on for ten more days, downriver and cross-country in bitter cold, standing guard through the nights, until he found a sheriff. He handed his prisoners over to the law. Much exertion, even manic bravado, on behalf of the idea of justice.

Later Roosevelt explained, "In any wild country, where the power of the law is little felt or heeded, and where everyone has to rely upon himself for protection, men soon get to feel that it is in the highest degree unwise to submit to any wrong without making immediate and resolute effort to avenge it upon the wrongdoers."

People in other countries sometimes accuse Americans of acting with "cowboy" logic. Yasser Arafat said as much when American fighters intercepted the Egyptian airliner carrying terrorists who had hijacked the *Achille Lauro* cruise ship in 1985. Arafat was right, in a way, about the cowboy logic. But his understanding of the word *cowboy* and an American's understanding of it are completely different. Arafat meant the word as an indictment. Americans might take it as a compliment. They might be delighted that they had been able to do a "cowboy" thing.

The archetypal cowboy is the leading man in the American collective unconscious. What Americans carry in their minds is not the historical reality of the cowboy but the myth as it came to them in books and movies, the cowboy according to Zane Grey and John Wayne. Americans, tutored in the lore from childhood, unconsciously see cowboy stories as morality plays. Good guys do battle with bad guys. In the American understanding of the myth, cowboys may sometimes operate outside the law or in the absence of the law, but they represent justice.

Gene Autry, a movie cowboy of the generation that always looked amazingly well-laundered, their white hats refulgently creamy, once formulated the "Ten Commandments of the Cowboy." They included injunctions to help people in distress, to tell the truth, to be "kind to small children, old folks and animals" and to "respect womanhood." The cowboy image got dirtier and more ambiguous in the era of Clint Eastwood, perhaps, but the persona remained heroic.

The rest of the world does not share Americans' sympathy for cowboys. Beyond the territorial waters, "cowboy" is often a term of derision, of contempt. In Europe, the word frequently conjures up everything that people fear and mistrust about Americans. It suggests unpredictable, violent behavior, a heedless and cavalier lawlessness and a kind of strenuous stupidity: a hard killer glint in the American eye, the loose cannon rolling around in the American mind. Vietnam was an American cowboy adventure that turned into a nightmare—cowboys and Indians, with the Indians at last driving the cowboys out into the South China Sea. The cowboy image does not always travel well abroad. It works best on the native range.

There was something both hilarious and sinister about Henry Kissinger's idea of himself as a cowboy. He told an Italian interviewer, Oriana Fallaci, that he saw himself as a lone gunman walking into town at high noon to impose order. The image of Kissinger standing there in the dust, Kissinger in cowboy boots and white cowboy hat, Kissinger with his soft white hand twitching toward his holster, is wondrous.

Teddy Roosevelt could play the part. He *was* a cowboy as a young man. He also went to Harvard and wrote books. Ronald Reagan, conservative and ex-movie actor, became "*Ronnie le cowboy*" in France even before he came to Washington, and the term was not one of endearment. Once Reagan became president, Europeans came to see, presiding over the nuclear button, the fate of the world, this cowboy, this actor of cowboys. The half-awakened image they had in mind came from the last few minutes of the movie *Dr. Strangelove*: Slim Pickens clutching his cowboy hat astride the falling H-bomb, whooping it up, riding "cowboy logic" down the air to global cinders. "We'll meet again, don't know where, don't know when . . . ."

And yet Europeans love cowboy books and cowboy movies. Whatever their official distaste for the cowboy mind-set, and however they censure the romantic recklessness, they often harbor a sneaking admiration of the individualism and freedom that the idea of the cowboy implies.

When Europeans, or Americans for that matter, think of the mythic American cowboy, the state where he lives is undoubtedly Texas.

The sheep men gathered at dusk outside the meeting hall in Mertzon, Texas. Each wore a cowboy hat (each hat distinctive, matching the weathered face) and an enormous belt buckle, the size of a Roman's shield. They stood in dusty boots on the scrubby grass and drank strong black coffee out of plastic cups as the night came on.

I had driven out to Mertzon from San Angelo with Elmer Kelton, an editor of *Livestock Weekly.* Kelton, who looks a little like Harry Truman and has the same erect bearing and American plain style of speech, is a novelist. His novels are always set in west Texas, and they are written in a prose that is a fairly precise stylistic equivalent of the west Texas landscape, large and open and slightly brusque, but with an arid grace.

Now Kelton moved among the ranchers gathered for the annual dinner of the West Texas Wool and Mohair Association. He bantered with them in the sidelong west Texas way, good-humored insult frisking just at the edges of the talk, like a sheepdog nipping at the fleecier pleasantries.

"Roy," Elmer would say. "How you? You all right?" It sounded, in the west Texas accent, like "Hah yew? Yew aw rat?"

It was a bad time then. The men talked, shaking their heads, about the economic disaster in the oil fields, about drill rigs selling for the price of scrap metal in Midland, the glass-and-steel mirage of a city that oil money had built in the boom times of the Permian basin. The smaller wells, called strippers, would be closing down all over Texas, the ranchers thought, and would be too expensive to start up again when the oil bust was over. "Then the tent makers will have it all," said one sheep man.

The collapse of oil had reverberated over the territory. Most of the ranchers leased land to the oil companies for drilling. Their royalty checks had shriveled. The startling fossil smell of oil, a reek of the inner earth uncorked, still blew in the air now and then, but many of the pump jacks that brought up the oil from the range, like blackbirds metronomically beaking the dust, were now motionless.

Things were coming up dry. The mesquite had its lovely light-green springtime leafing just then — a touch of almost Japanese delicacy in a rough, dun-colored country — but mesquite is a thirsty parasite, a drinker with deep roots that steal water from the rest of the landscape. Mesquite was for grilling meats for young lawyers and bankers in New York and Los Angeles. Livestock could not live on it. The range grass was sparse now among the limestone and caliche. The herds would need to be culled, the lambs taken off the ewes early and sold to save money on feed. It looked like a dusty summer coming. I had been out on the range the day before with a rancher friend of mine, Hal Noelke, and his kinsman, E.L. Tankersley. They were both descended from the first cattleman in Tom Green County. E.L. was marking sheep (removing their testicles and the tips of their tails), and during the day he killed the first rattlesnake of the season — small, but frisky: seven rattles.

Elmer Kelton and I drifted inside the hall with the sheep men and joined the line for the chicken-fried steak and corn on the cob and white bread that looked as if it had been cut in thick slices off a loaf of cotton. Chicken-fried steak is a regular item of Texas fare — a slab of beef batter-fried. The joke on the rube from the North is that he came to Texas and ordered chicken-fried steak, rare — the joke being that the meat is always cooked the same way. Chicken-fried steak can be delicious, but the ranchers this year were regretting that the Wool and Mohair Association was not serving its usual wonderful barbecue. Hell of a note, they agreed, mock rueful, as if this were the last straw in a bad year.

Then an officer of the association came to the microphone at the head of the hall and called for attention. The ranchers stood at their long tables, removed their cowboy hats and bowed their heads and prayed for rain.

Texas was celebrating its 150th anniversary that year — not its 150th anniversary as a state, but the 150th anniversary of its founding as an independent republic. That independence is one of the reasons for the Texas mystique. Texans are uniquely Texans, and that makes them quintessentially American in a way that no other group is. It is hard to imagine a man from Chicago calling himself an Illinoisan, for example, in the way that a man from Dallas will call himself a Texan. The same year that Texas celebrated its sesquicentennial, Arkansas celebrated the centennial of its statehood, but few outside Arkansas noticed.

Texas is a state with strong flavors and themes and a distinct identity. The Texan's ancestral memory is strong. The state's highways are lined with historical markers that recite the state's lore in minute detail. The roads are also lined with antilittering signs that sound just the right note of truculent nationalism: DON'T MESS WITH TEXAS.

Texans cherish a sort of dual citizenship. They joke about it. Lone Star calls itself the "national" beer of Texas. During better times, someone proposed starting a society to build a six-foot-high wall around Texas to keep out carpetbagging Yankees. But as the economy of Texas faltered with the collapse of oil prices, a lot of the Yankee immigrants started heading back north.

The rhythms of boom or bust are part of the mystique of Texas. A Texas historian named Joe Frantz remarked: "Texans are not like the Yankee who puts his money in the bank and collects compound interest. We take risks. And when it doesn't pan out, we don't blame a man. Going broke is not an occasion for gloom. It just means you are short of cash."

Texas is a complicated place psychologically. In one way, it is (improbably) like Japan: nearly everything that one can say about Texas can be countered with an opposite and equally true assertion. Not quite: If you say Texas is big, you cannot also say that Texas is small. But if you say Texas is historically glorious, you can also say that Texas has been ugly and mean, a place full of violence and fire ants and rattlesnakes.

Texas history has been heroic, and yet Sam Houston, when he lived among the Cherokees, was known as Big Drunk. Texas is rich, but also desperately poor and hardscrabble. If you say Texas is ruggedly individualistic, you can also say it is meritlessly lucky to be built on top of a vast natural oil tank. If you say that Texas is full of self-confident brag, it is also true that Texans are often insecure (no contradiction, perhaps). Texas has a sort of inferiority-superiority complex, it may be.

One of the charms of Texas is its inherent exaggeration of almost everything. Its weather runs to violent extremes. It is a rough joke to survive a drought of several years and then find the dry spell broken by torrential rains that can flood the town and wash away the pickup truck. Texas humor, like the Texas landscape, accommodates outrageous possibilities.

"Well," said Monte Noelke, another member of the tribe, "there was a man named Fenstermacher who came from up North some place, and bought some land around here. The first night he was out here, a couple of cowboys decided to impress him a little. So when it came time to go to bed in the little bunkhouse over there, one of the cowboys said good night to Fenstermacher and then pulled out his pistol and shot out the light."

As if to say, that's the way we put out the lights down here in Texas.

That is Texas humor. In an outrageously physical way, the Texan contrives to confirm an outsider's expectations so that the joke on the Texan (Texans are crude, you know, and they carry six-shooters) is turned into a joke on the outlander who believes the buffoonery of local color staged for his benefit. Texans love to play Texan, and then some, for the benefit of non-Texans.

Lyndon Johnson was forever playing Texan—wheedling, pawing, telling Texas stories. It was his style: shrewd, funny and complicated. It worked in Texas, and it worked in the U.S. Senate. Johnson's complex manipulations of the truth, his capework with fact and illusion and expectation, all derived, I thought, from a perfectly Texan source: an ancestral knowledge that you cannot survive in the world, and certainly not in Texas, without aggressively taking hold of everything you can, including a man's mind and credulity, and bending it, working it to your will, the country being too tough for anything less.

But the Kennedys, and the people around them, never got the joke, never thought that Texas was all that endearing. It was a source of gall to Johnson that after John Kennedy's assassination, the late president's family and his friends and loyalists all found Johnson crude and grotesque and buffoonish. The Texan in the Texas joke is supposed to

have the last laugh because he is satirizing his own alleged buffoonery.
But with the Kennedys, Johnson never had the last laugh, and I suspect it
embittered and confused him.

Robert Straus, the former chairman of the Democratic National Committee, is a Texan with bardic gifts. I heard him once tell a quintessential
Lyndon Johnson story. Straus went down to the LBJ Ranch in the Texas
hill country one day to call on Johnson. LBJ was out of the White House
then. In essence, he had been driven out of the presidency by the turmoil
that was loose in America, by the war and the antiwar protests, by the
memorable hatreds that went jolting through the country.

Johnson had gone back to Texas to die. He had let his hair grow long —
a strange, poignant detail, a sort of plea, I thought. Or else, what? His
tormenters, the great American counterculture, wore their hair long, and
now Johnson imitated them, but why? To detoxify himself? To capitulate
somehow to his own destroyers? He had started to smoke cigarettes
again, a habit he had given up in the fifties after his heart attacks.

So Straus came to see LBJ at the ranch. He found Lyndon talking with a
preacher in the living room. Johnson and the preacher were matter-of-
factly going over the eulogy that the preacher would deliver over
Johnson's grave. Johnson was briskly editing his own funeral sermon.

Johnson motioned for Straus to take a chair. Then he signaled for the
preacher to continue.

The preacher, with great preacherly roundness of phrase, began:
"Lyndon Johnson — a simple man! A man of the soil!"

Lyndon cut him off abruptly. "No, no, no, no!" Then Lyndon assumed
the preacherly tone himself and spoke the correct version: "Lyndon
Johnson, statesman! World leader!" And so on.

Lyndon Johnson, who had spent his life manipulating and controlling,
pulling the levers of power, now sought — whatever his self-destructive
trajectory — to stage-manage his own funeral. He could not help himself.
Even when he wanted to die — as he probably did, since a man with a

history of heart attacks does not start smoking again—the irrepressibly conniving Texan in him could not subside.

The most attractive part of the spirit of Texas, I think, has to do with that powerful life force. What is best about Texas is more generally what is best about America — a talent for being very much alive.

Monte and I were wandering around his Double Half Circle ranch in a pickup truck. The sun went down in a sweet clarity of vanishing light, and we saw stars above the enormous landscape even before the colors of the day were gone.

Monte is an esteemed storyteller locally, a funny man with a cross-grained sense of humor and an undercurrent of melancholy. It is said that all of the Noelkes are characters. The ones I know are.

Monte was living now in the house where he grew up. Like most west Texas ranch houses, it was built on one story and was resolutely unpretentious. West Texans, unlike people from Dallas or Houston, regard ostentation as absurd. "Everyone knows who you are," they say. "There is no need to show it."

The west Texas ranch house usually has a few items of Western art — an oil painting of cattle, a pseudo-Remington bronze of cowboys on horseback. Monte's living room had a bronze that his son had done. Monte's house also sported many books. He is a restless reader.

One of the charms of Texas is its talent to surprise. I was astonished to find that Monte had become a fine cook. He was divorced and lived alone, and went aggressively at mastering the thing. He served a four-course dinner. We started with pâté with capers. I don't think Monte could claim credit for that. Then we had a wonderful cold leek soup that Monte had made. Then a salad, which Monte got the recipe for at a restaurant in Versailles. Then came the steak — grass-fed and charcoal grilled. Then strawberries and apples, and espresso. Monte and I were a long way from the chuck wagon.

We talked for a long time, about marriages, for example. We talked about memory — what it is necessary to remember and what it is necessary to forget. We talked about the Holocaust and the moralities of remembering, and about the work of Elie Wiesel.

There was a deep conflict there, I thought. The American mind, the Texas mind, tends to be vigorously oblivious. It is useful to forget, for the past is dead weight, and the American needs to get moving.

My own inclination is to remember obsessively — to indulge the past at the expense of present and future. Perhaps it is a writer's trait.

When we walked outside after dinner, there was a full moon, and the stars were crystals against the black sky. I drove back to San Angelo — the first twenty-three miles of the trip on Monte's unpaved ranch road. Everywhere there were jackrabbits — hundreds of jackrabbits, leaping and dancing and skittering. Soon my car was skittering too, as I swerved to avoid them. At length, I turned off the headlights, which turned off the jackrabbits, and I navigated across the range by moonlight.

Back in San Angelo I could not sleep. I dressed again and walked downstairs in the Sheraton to Pepper's Lounge, where I ordered a beer. A country band was playing. The dance floor was filled with couples doing the Cotton-Eye Joe. The men were dancing with their cowboy hats on, wearing jeans and western shirts. The men moved with a sly, sinuous motion, a motion economical and almost surreptitious. A snaky motion. Their feet stayed close to the floor. Their knees and hips did the moving — as if, I thought, they were riding horseback and the lower body was answering to an invisible horse beneath them.

The man looked aside and downward as he danced, as if abstracted.
The woman, if she did not know her partner well, would hold her hand
with the back of her thumb lightly against his back or shoulder as she
danced, as if not to give him too much of the heat of her palm.

The Texas Two-Step and the Cotton-Eye Joe. They are not sexual
dances exactly, but they are not unsexual either.

Every night in Pepper's Lounge there was an eighty-year-old man who
came to dance, a tough old bird in white shirt and dark tie and dark blue
trousers. He was wizened down to something just over five feet tall, but
he danced all evening, for hours, snatching up any unoccupied woman,
old or young, and sliding energetically around the floor with her until the
music stopped. Then he dropped her and went prowling for another. The
women were good about it and treated him like a young man, which in
some essential way he was. I learned later that he came from a nursing
home a few blocks away and was a local phenomenon.

The Texas mystique has something to do with freedom, individualism,
independence, fearlessness, self-sufficiency and high-school football.
A Texas proverb says: "Great country for men and dogs, but hell on
women and horses." Texas is essentially a masculine society, I suppose,
although I found myself enormously fond of Texas women, who seemed
to me spirited and able and very funny.

The Texas historian T.R. Fehrenbach, in a wonderful phrase, writes of
"a barbarian awareness of true danger." Texans remind Americans of
their earlier selves, their more vigorous and independent selves. Texas
reminds Americans of the moment, irrecoverable, when the barbarian
self, physical, alert, free, intersected with the housebroken citizen. What
Americans love about Texas is the barbarian awareness, and a sense
that life can be simple and direct and physical and spacious.

Texas has been an idealized anachronism of the American character. During much of the twentieth century, Texas remained a nineteenth-century society. Texas was neither industrial nor mercantile, and it was isolated from the rest of the nation — standing in a sense alone, as it had as a republic. The speech of Texans was distinct and vivid. Texas was exuberantly and arrogantly parochial. It was endlessly spacious, and yet enclosed. The land had its moments of loveliness, but was otherwise too demanding, even vicious, to indulge a passive character. Life was struggle.

Kit Carson, nineteenth-century trapper, guide and soldier, was succinct about the primal American journeying: "The cowards never started, and the weak died on the way."

Gus Clemens and I sat for a long time over lunch at Fuentes Restaurant in San Angelo. Gus is a west Texas historian. He remembered the terrible drought of the fifties when he was a child.

"Every Sunday in church," he said, "we prayed for rain. If you don't take the long view out here, you just don't make it. You appreciate the land over the decades, not over the seasons." He allowed himself an instant of eloquence: "This is a stern land." Then he returned to Fuentes's cooking, which is the best in San Angelo.

After lunch I found Elmer Kelton at the offices of *Livestock Weekly* — out Beauregard, across from the junior high school — and talked to him about the Texas mystique. He regarded it mostly as nonsense.

"Those who struck it big manufactured the folklore and the myth," said Kelton. "People go back into history and exaggerate the romance. The early days of Texas were hardscrabble, close to disaster. It was no paradise in the times we are celebrating now.

"My people were cow people for three generations back. Low pay. Hard work. But there was a lot of pride in being good at what a man did.

Not like the movies. There was pride in horsemanship. They judged each other by that more than anything else."

The ranchers still use horses sometimes. But it is easier to coax cattle into the corral using a pickup truck and a feed sack — the artfully dribbling feed sack enticing the cows along.

In any case, a man really can't make money in cattle anymore. Americans do not eat enough beef; they are worried about cholesterol. Ranchers survive on outside income. They get royalties for the mineral rights on their lands. They take a job in town. They lease some land to deer hunters. Some ranchers even import animals from Africa — impala, cape buffalo, gazelles — and advertise Texas safaris.

I like to drive out of San Angelo, past Mertzon, to visit Hal Noelke. He has the odd family sense of humor. He is a big man who affects a Texas crudity as a personal style, but he is literate, intelligent and kind. Like many of these ranchers, he travels widely, and when he is abroad, I suspect, he never fails to play the Texan. When I came to visit him last time, he brought along a copy of an essay I had written for *Time* magazine. He had circled a couple of big words, and he thrust the page in front of me, challenging me: "Come on, Lance. Well, gawddamn!" As an editor, he was right. I should not have used the words.

That night I stayed at Hal's ranch, sleeping on the fold-out couch in the living room. We had stayed up late with E.L. Tankersley, drinking a tequila that Hal liked and talking about Texas history.

In the morning, I walked into the kitchen for breakfast. A peacock was screaming outside. Hal and I looked out the window at the same time, and saw that his two sheepdogs were copulating in the yard.

Hal contemplated them with disgust and said, "Now, come on, boys, gawd dangit! We got company!"

Previous pages: *Long before the Europeans arrived, the native people raised sheep on the western lands.*

Left: *The Spanish influence is still seen in the Southwest, much of which was once part of Mexico. The Ranchos de Taos in New Mexico is a national historical landmark.*

Right: *An influence of another sort: the neon lights of Las Vegas attract gamblers to the city's famous casinos and nightclubs.*

Left: "Ride 'em, cowboy." A rider at
Frontier Days in Cheyenne, Wyoming,
top show on the rodeo circuit. Saddle-
bronco riding, the most popular rodeo
event, requires the contestant to stay
aboard for a minimum of eight seconds
while holding a single rein and spurring
the bucking horse.

Right top: Disco, western style: the
Texas Two-Step and Cotton-Eye Joe.

Right below: Boys watch the rodeo and
await their turn.

Previous pages: *Driving through Texas takes as long as crossing entire European nations. Arriving in Houston makes the trip worthwhile. The largest city in the state, it was named after Sam Houston and served as the capital of the Republic of Texas in the mid-1800s.*

Left: *A highway snakes across the western landscape.*

Right: *Rugged California scenery.*

Wind and rain have carved the bleak landscape of Utah into striking formations. Much of the state is covered by desert.

Right: *Saloons in cattle towns were roisterous places for drinking and gambling. They provided a welcome respite for hardworking cowhands who had often spent months on the trail.*

Above: *Hired ranch hands in the late nineteenth century, cowboys have become immortalized by myth and Hollywood as knights of the Old West, men of few words and high morals. The image of the tough individualist in the white hat has become tarnished lately, but the legend lives on.*

Left: *The rodeo clown is not there only to entertain. He is ready to distract the bull if the rider falls.*

Previous pages: *A lone rider surveys a seemingly endless wilderness.*

Below: *In the background the city encroaches on land that for almost 300 years belonged to herds of longhorns. These cattle, descendants of bulls and cows brought to Mexico by Spanish conquistadors, roamed wild on the Texas prairies until the 1800s.*

Once it was their land, now the Navajo, like other native people, live on reservations or have become assimilated into American society.

WE THE PEOPLE

Like a modern version of American Gothic, a couple pose by the farm.

A presidential campaign is a phenomenon of surreal trajectories.

The German shepherds working for the Secret Service frisk around and smell our luggage, searching for explosives, and then we climb aboard the candidate's plane. The plane rises out of the weather, out of the noise and scurry and disorder of one campaign stop, and breaks into pure sunshine. We fly through the blue altitudes, over the abstract, tumbling snowfields of cumulus. Then we plunge down again, into the weather, into another city, into another part of America. Pittsburgh. Raleigh. Oakland. Milwaukee.

The United States ceases to be a geographic continuum. It becomes, instead, a sequence of fragmented locales, discrete and (except for hurriedly noticed details of local color) interchangeable, like particles in Albert Einstein's physics. The political gods ascend and descend with their entourages and motorcades. They sweep to the event—the rally, the convention, the union conference, the grand opening, whatever—and then sweep back to the plane and away.

It is always touching and a little haunting to see the people waiting on the access roads for the motorcade to hurry by, waiting for an hour or two in little clusters, holding signs of support or hostility, waiting for a glimpse that lasts a few seconds, a glimpse mainly of limousines surrounded by screaming police motorcycles and followed by two or three chartered Greyhound buses bearing the press. Once in a while, for an instant, they will make out the candidate (in this year, Walter Mondale or Ronald Reagan), or a part of the candidate—a flash of smiling profile, a waving palm. The sight is haunting because those people, receding in the distance, always look as if they have just been abandoned there by the roadside.

A presidential campaign is a strange, rather interesting way to see America's cities. For a couple of weeks during the fall of 1984, I traveled with the Mondale and Reagan campaigns, switching back and forth from one to the other, which made the exercise doubly surreal.

The trip gave me a new respect for the energy and variety of American cities, and for their complexity. The cities by definition are the antithesis of the western ideal in America. The Texas myth is spacious and untrammeled; a man out there had a sense of his freedom in the large landscape. The cities are the American densities, its bundles of ethnic concentration, its industrial powers and sometimes its depressed decays.

One day the Mondale campaign descended upon Pittsburgh for a labor rally in the heart of the downtown district. Sleek, new skyscrapers of dark glass rose there, and yet the steelworkers and other laborers assembled were not feeling sleek. The American steel industry had been shutting down for years, unable to compete with the Japanese and others in the world market. The steelworkers were bitterly angry at what had become of their once triumphal industry. They felt betrayed and abandoned.

In the American cities one sees the complex layerings of American time — squat turn-of-the-century neighborhoods with filigreed stonework and woodwork lie in the shadows of extraterrestrial geometries of glass and steel. The cities have risen a little hectically. In the older cities — Boston, Chicago, San Francisco — historical times and architectural styles leapfrog one another. Some of the old Boston gets smashed down to make way for a bright new architecture, which then will coexist with remnant slums and the graceful houses of Beacon Hill.

American cities have shown a remarkable resilience. Not many years ago the cities of the Northeast, for example, were reading their own obituaries. The nation's moral and financial energy had departed for the Sunbelt, it was said, for Houston and Phoenix and Tucson and San Diego. But cities like Baltimore and Boston and Albany and Philadelphia at least in part revived themselves, often handsomely.

The cities are always densely complicated. I know New York better than other American cities because I have lived there a long time. There are moments when New York is perfect. New Yorkers collect these moments and savor them in small private flashes of recall:

- The hour before dusk on a clear day in mid-December when the air holds a pure, cold light and one walks south on Fifth Avenue toward the Plaza Hotel, the Christmas decorations bright in the coming winter twilight, the sidewalks alive with shoppers, the world crisp and crystalline. Twin clouds of breath burst from the nostrils of the carriage horses.
- The afternoon in mid-October (red and golden leaves, deep blue sky) when one takes a vendor-cart hot dog and lemonade to the boat pond in Central Park to watch white-sailed model boats heeling stiffly in the breeze, guided by intense men and boys on the shore who wave the antennas of their electronic remote controls like wands.
- Almost any time that one beholds the Brooklyn Bridge, but especially on the night of a full moon, the bridge's splendid webbing glittering, the whole masterpiece giving off an eerie thrum, which is the sound of rubber tires on the grid work of the bridge's roadway.

In his movies, Woody Allen sets such moments to George Gershwin's music. The city is Woody Allen's instrument, and he plays it tenderly.

But New York is never merely exquisite for very long. New York, being a great city — powerful, passionate and crass, a world capital of finance and trade, of art and culture — is too compacted and turbulent, too neurotic and messy and erratically brilliant and mean to be turned into a procession of metropolitan haiku.

Limousines hurtle down the avenues. Illegal aliens labor in the sweatshops of the Bronx. The New Yorker's mind takes in the city's crystal moments, and its squalor too: the homeless people crumpled in doorways, the subway cars covered with graffiti like the symptoms of a disease.

Sometimes the two elements intermingle. Late on a summer night in an apartment just below East Harlem, I heard the city's night sounds: the stray cherry bomb, the car's break-in alarm that whoops like an outraged jungle bird, the ambulance sirens wailing off toward an emergency room. But then across the air shaft, through hot motionless air, someone's piano poured out Mozart like the brightest ice water, a flow of pure intelligence.

The Manichaeans of the third century believed that Satan coexists with God. New York is a Manichaean town.

One night during the summer when the New York Mets won the National League pennant, I rode the subway out to Shea Stadium to watch them play a baseball game against the Chicago Cubs.

It was about six-thirty in the evening. People were heading home from work. I studied the faces in the subway in some astonishment. My friend Rob Cowley and I had the only white faces in the subway car. The others were shades of black and brown and yellow — the new America. There were Vietnamese and Pakistanis, Latin Americans, Filipinos, Chinese, Japanese, Lebanese, Iranians — on and on.

The kinetic energy of new combinations is changing America today as profoundly as it did at the turn of the century, when the great migrations came through Ellis Island from eastern and southern Europe. Now the new immigrants get off their jets and stream through customs at Kennedy Airport. Sometimes, they scramble up across the border near San Ysidro, California, in the middle of the night, or they arrive in the trunks of cars, or they wash up in foundering boats on the Florida Keys.

Native-born Americans are ambivalent about the new arrivals. Ambivalence is what old Americans have always felt about new Americans. At times it was something worse than ambivalence. In 1751 Benjamin Franklin asked, "Why should the Palatine boors be suffered to swarm into our settlements, and by herding together, establish their language and manners, to the exclusion of ours? Why should Pennsylvania, founded by the English, become a colony of aliens, who will shortly be so numerous as to Germanize us, instead of our Anglifying them?"

At a remove of several generations from Ellis Island, some sentimentalize the immigrant experience. They project their nostalgia upon today's immigrants and wish them well. But the native-born also feel the alien vibration. *Alien* is a dank and sinister word — the ominous otherness, not our kind. A flickering fear arises that America is being overrun. Racism in new combinations jounces around.

The new immigrants form an insistent presence. A single cluster of fourteen brown-brick stores in New York City harbors a Korean beauty parlor, a Chinese hardware store, a South Asian spice shop, a Chinese watch store and a Korean barber. At a high school on Chicago's far North Side, algebra classes are conducted not only in English, but in Spanish, Cantonese, Vietnamese and Assyrian.

In a sense, America long ago made a shrewd instinctive bargain with the world. It offered a prize — its wealth, its freedom and promise — and then, Darwinian, it dared those strong enough and bold enough to make the leap. It was, and is, a hard journey. And of course the newcomers were sometimes too literal-minded about the prize. The sidewalks were not paved with gold.

Sentimentally, one thinks that it was America, really, that got the prize — the enormous energy unleashed by the immigrant dislocations. Immigrants bring a formidable capacity for work. Having to work to stay alive, to build a future, gives one's exertions a tough moral simplicity.

Edward Kennedy told a story of how, during his first campaign for the Senate, his opponent said scornfully during a debate: "This man has never worked a day in his life!" Kennedy says that the next morning, as he was shaking hands at a factory gate, one worker leaned toward him and muttered: "You ain't missed a goddamn thing!"

Americans harbor complex prejudices and ideologies about work. For a time during the seventies, there were lamentations that the old American work ethic had died, and there were answering lamentations that work was brutalizing, stultifying, imprisoning. In his 1972 book *Working*, Studs Terkel began: "This book, being about work, is, by its very nature, about violence — to the spirit as well as to the body." The historical horrors of industrialization (child labor, Dickensian squalor, the dark satanic mills) translated into the twentieth century's robotic busywork on the line, tightening the same damned screw on the fire-wall assembly, going nuts to the banging, jangling Chaplinesque din of modern materialism at work.

Of course, in patchwork, pluralistic America, different classes and ethnic groups stand at different stages in the hierarchies of work. The immigrants, legal and illegal, are fighting for the foothold that more leisurely Americans may have achieved three generations ago. The Koreans who run the vegetable markets, or Vietnamese boat people trying to open a restaurant, or Chicanos who struggle to start a small business in the barrio are still years away from backpacking and windsurfing.

Thomas Carlyle, the Scottish historian, thought that "all work, even cotton spinning, is noble; work is alone noble." Of course, it is seigneurial cant to romanticize work that is detestable or destructive to workers. But Americans are a little spoiled on the subject of work. The preindustrial peasant and the nineteenth-century American farmer did brutish work far harder than that done on the assembly line. In Nicaragua, the average nineteen-year-old peasant has worked longer and harder than most Americans of middle age.

Nevertheless, work is still the core of most Americans' lives; the occupation is melded to the identity. Freud said that the successful psyche is one capable of love and of work. Work is probably the most thorough and profound organizing principle of American life. Mobility weakens American blood ties, and often, Americans' coworkers form their new family, tribe and social world. A worker becomes almost a citizen of the company, living under the protection of salaries, pensions, health insurance. Some sociologists think that people like jobs mainly because they need other people, need to gossip with them, hang out with them. The job performs the function of community.

Still, it occurs to me sometimes that the old American genius for work is in some ways being replaced by a genius for leisure. The stages of civilization. The Japanese now have the genius for work. Americans are brilliant at their diversions.

Americans have a tribal sense of occasions, which they invent with extravagant ingenuity. And television allows them to proliferate the occasions, to distribute them everywhere, so that the Superbowl or the World Series becomes a vast participatory spectacle. As do American political conventions and campaigns, which are elaborate circuses of sentiment and persuasion.

The 1984 Olympic Games were a masterpiece of that sort of American spectacle. They were an American ceremony that connected leisure and athletic competition to national politics and morale. The Olympics dramatized a shift in American values.

From the beginning, American sentiment has been torn between the values of freedom and equality. Under Franklin Roosevelt, and for several generations afterward, the official American inclination was toward equality. In the eighties, the value of freedom reasserted itself, sometimes harshly and at the expense of compassionate instincts. The Olympics expressed the preference perfectly: the freedom to win — athletics as Darwinian theater.

"Nothing great was ever achieved without enthusiasm," Ralph Waldo Emerson wrote. The Los Angeles Olympics were staged, God knows, with enthusiasm — even a triumphal gloating that justifiably irritated many people around the world. A professor of public policy at Duke University,

Carol Stack, watched the spectacle and said, "It's almost like the old Ghost Dances that the Indians used to go through in hopes they could bring back what they had lost. Americans today are performing their own version of the ghost dance, only it's not being called a ghost dance anymore. It is called being patriotic."

In any case, grand spectacles in America often serve a sort of sacramental purpose — to dramatize a state of mind, or even to create a state of mind. Woodstock served such a purpose.

On the other hand, what is the sacramental purpose of the Indianapolis 500 or of a Willie Nelson concert? Americans are a gregarious people.

New Orleans and jazz: a magical combination. The city gave birth to the music in the early 1900s, and since then musicians have developed and refined the form in bars and nightclubs in the French Quarter.

Previous pages: *Superman floats above a Macy's Thanksgiving Day parade in New York, ready to swoop down and defend truth, justice and the American way.*

Left: *Commuters in New York City.*

Workers head home at the end of day.

Left top: *A woman waits at San Geronimo de Taos, a village established by Pueblo Indians about 1000 A.D.*

Left below: *Poverty and crime are among New Orleans' chief social problems.*

Below: *"Where did he go?" Army personnel scan their surroundings through binoculars.*

Left: Bright colors and loud music: a stadium crowd can be as interesting as the main event.

Above: *Making music: a band of senior citizens in San Antonio, Texas, catches the beat.*

Previous pages: *Cheerleaders practice for the big game.*

Left: *Busy shoppers at South Street Seaport in New York City search for the freshest catch.*

Right: *Choosing just the right pumpkin for the Halloween jack-o'-lantern takes time and skill.*

Left: *Early in the nineteenth century Coney Island, New York, was an elite resort. Later in the century it became one of the most colorful and lively amusement parks in the country. Since the Second World War it has become a more conventional recreation area, but still attracts thousands—especially on sultry summer weekends when the towels cover every inch of sand.*

Right: *White water canoeing is a sport that combines adventure, skill and sight-seeing—but don't take your eyes off the rocks ahead for too long.*

Below: *A woman tends a springhouse in Virginia.*

Previous pages: *Immigrants continue to come to America, drawn by the promise of freedom and the possibility of wealth. In exchange they bring their determination and skills and the richness of their cultures.*

Left: *The stark lines of the World Trade Center and the uniformity of the business community reflect one side of New York.*

Right: *The clutter and vitality of this diner and the nonchalance of its patrons are equally a part of the Big Apple.*

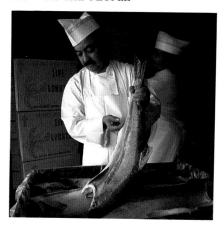

Left: *Getting the fish ready for market.*

Below: *Fishing in Hawaii.*

Right: *Thanksgiving dinner is an important American tradition.*

Below: *A calf-judging contest at a country fair in New York State.*

Left: *Navajo boy.*

Below: *Young dancers.*

Right: *Eskimo child.*

Above: *Baseball fans.*

Previous pages: *Students at the Citadel, a liberal arts military college in Charleston, South Carolina, wear uniforms and sleep in barracks.*

Two country and western musicians play the fiddle and guitar, the traditional instruments of this form of music, which traces its roots back to Anglo and Celtic immigrants who preserved their ballads and folksongs. The addition of instrumental accompaniment was a major factor in the transition of this folk music to a pop form.

Right: *Performers at Washington Square Park at the foot of Fifth Avenue in New York City. This public park is the heart of Greenwich Village.*

Eskimo drummers in Alaska perform drum dance songs. The men beat on membrane-covered drums with long slender sticks while the women dance and sing.

Right: *Pro football is watched mostly from the easy chair. Television has greatly increased the sport's popularity. The Super Bowl is now the most popular televised event in the United States.*

Above: *What better activity for a sunny autumn day than cheering for a football team?*

The loneliness of the long-distance skier: the start of a cross-country ski race in Telemark, Wisconsin.

Right: *Donald Duck greets a small admirer in Disneyland, an amusement park in Anaheim, California, designed by Walt Disney. Its attractions include a fairyland castle and a jungle boat ride.*

Below: *Chicagoans gather at the Grant Park Band Shell for free summer concerts. The park, between Lake Michigan and the downtown, offers open spaces, fine museums, and the beautiful Buckingham Fountain.*

Left: *Men and women stand in an unemployment line.*

Right: *Red-faced from cold and exertion, a stevedore in Maine loads potatoes onto a ship.*

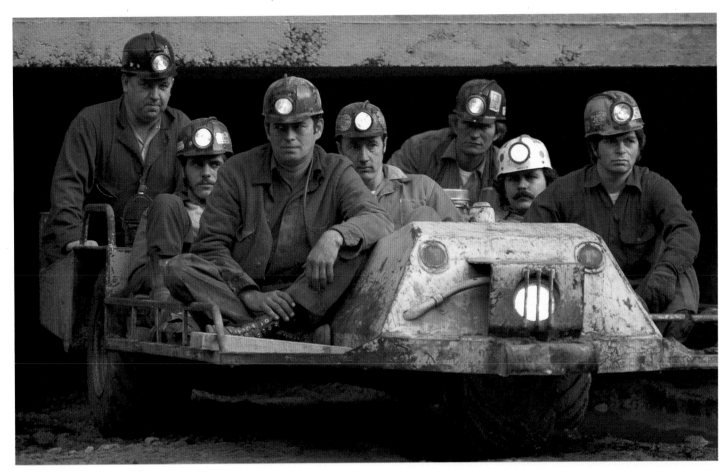

Above: *Coal miners in Kentucky.*

Left: *Woman at work.*

Right: *Fatherhood.*

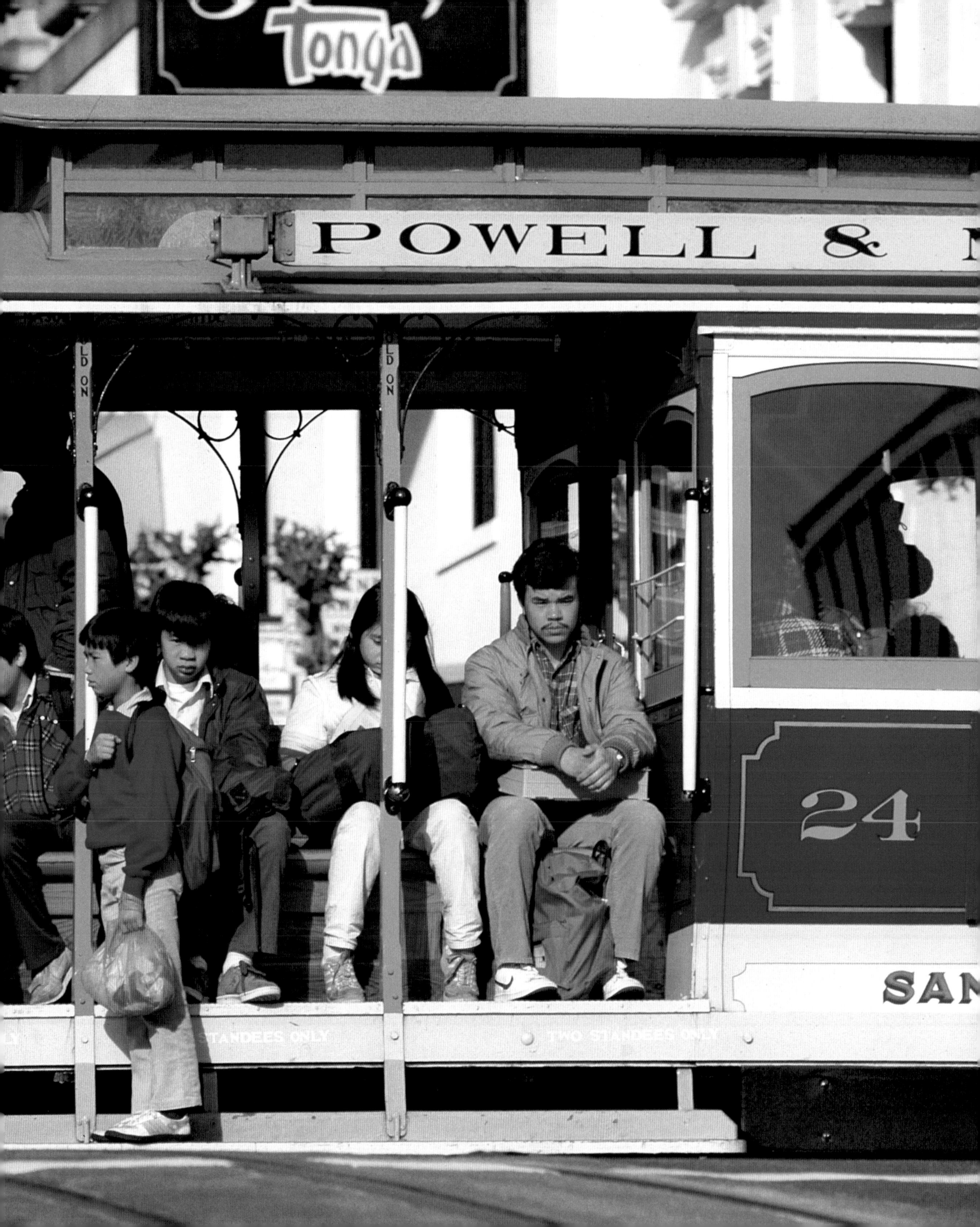
Tonga
POWELL & M
24
SAN
TWO STANDEES ONLY

Left: *The newsroom of a large urban newspaper hums with activity as journalists rush to finish their stories, but one sound once associated with the scene—the clatter of typewriters—has disappeared as computer terminals have taken over.*

Previous pages: *San Francisco's cable cars, designed for the city's steep hills, run on rails and are pulled by an endless steel cable beneath the street surface.*

Below: *Periods of massive immigration from China produced Chinatowns in many American cities. To this day many have retained their unique character.*

Participant in Kamehameha Day festivities in Kailua, Hawaii: a festival to honor King Kamehameha I, who united the islands for the first time in 1795 and founded the Kingdom of Hawaii.

A SENSE OF PLACE

Huge dunes of white gypsum sand form an arid wilderness at White Sand National Monument in southern New Mexico. The strange-looking yucca plant is an evergreen, which the Indians used to make sandals, mats and rope, and which they ate in winter.

It is difficult for me to see American landscapes without investing them with emotional resonances. America is its coastlines and mountains and forests, its midwestern farmlands and prairies, its Gulf Coast bayous and deep southern piney woods, its flat cow country, its hallucinatory painted deserts, its Rocky Mountains, its north woods. . . .

America, being an idea, has a powerful subjective existence. The significance of American places is not intrinsic, but derives from the wash of imagination across the continent. Even though the cities and main roads of America have, since the Second World War, lost some of their distinctive sense of place and become more standardized, cut from the same molds, the same commercial franchise logos, those interchangeable parts are still a relatively trivial portion of the country.

To an American, America vibrates in the mind as well as in the eye. Each American, depending upon where life has taken him or her, carries along in the mind certain American landscapes. Each landscape has a powerful and distinctive meaning. The sum of these meanings is America itself, and the sums are always changing, from generation to generation, decade to decade, even from president to president.

When Americans elect a president, they choose a version of America, an interpretation of the American idea. Often the choices offered are not particularly appetizing. Still, each American election is an act of national self-definition.

Ronald Reagan's version of America was brilliantly evoked. Reagan possessed a sort of genius for the styles of American memory, for the layerings of the American past. The writer Wright Morris once wrote of Norman Rockwell that "his special triumph is in the conviction his countrymen share that the mythical world he evokes actually exists. . . . He understands the hunger, and he supplies the nourishment. The hunger is for the Good Old Days—the black-eyed tomboy, the hopeless,

179

lovable pup, the frecklefaced young swain . . . sensations which we no longer have but still seem to want; dreams of innocence before it went corrupt." Reagan also understood the hunger. He was not cynical when he delved into the layers of American memory, for they are his own layers of memory.

Reagan's predecessors were as profoundly and regionally American as he: especially Lyndon Johnson, out of Texas, and Jimmy Carter, out of south Georgia. Even Richard Nixon carried Whittier, California, with him. Their pasts were all shadowed, in different ways, by some obscure hurt. (All of them had strong and drivingly ambitious mothers, as did Reagan.) Reagan was of a sunnier temperament. His father was an improvident alcoholic in Dixon, Illinois, and yet Reagan's mythic hometown America was a glorious place. Reagan communicated a bright and triumphant American past.

It was a curious American effect. The reality of Reagan's childhood was probably a tale of failure and funk out of Theodore Dreiser, author of *An American Tragedy.* But the myth, the memory of the time, seems like Booth Tarkington, like his novel of Penrod Schofield, an exuberant American small-town innocent. Reagan said that his was a "Tom Sawyer–Huck Finn childhood."

Saying that, he was airbrushing out of American memory the shadows of Mark Twain's work. *Huckleberry Finn* is the greatest American work about freedom. It is also a savage description of American ignorance and violence. Reagan remembered only the innocence.

Huck Finn's father was a vicious alcoholic. Reagan discusses his father's alcoholism only once in his autobiography, *Where Is the Rest of Me?* In that passage, Reagan describes coming home on a cold night and finding his father passed out on the porch. He had to carry the old man inside — and may have thus saved his life. But if it happened once, it happened many times. He must have seen his father drunk a great deal. Living in a small town, he also must have suffered the chronic humiliation of being the son of a notorious drunk. Everybody knew. Old man Reagan, they said, had a powerful thirst.

The children of alcoholics often respond to the ordeal by blotting from their minds the reality of such horrors, and the memory of them. Denial is the essence of alcoholism, and it is also often the essence of how the children of alcoholics cope with the ordeal. After all, the world that the alcoholic makes, and forces his family to inhabit as well, is filled with illusion. Reality is difficult to get hold of. By night, the father may be a raving besotted wild man, and next morning he might be someone entirely different. He may not even remember what he was and what he did the night before. Nobody says anything, and it is as if nothing happened, except that there is always that residue of poisonous strife in the air. Something *did* happen. Which is the reality? The father drunk or the father sober?

The children of alcoholics tend to shrink from threatening confrontations and from dangerous realities. Their response is to recoil, or to escape into another version, into a daydream.

Reagan became famous for telling anecdotes from movies — stories of war heroics, usually — as if he thought that they had actually happened in real life. He did the same for American myth; he effaced the memory of squalor and drunkenness and pain, and retailed a bright small-town America that was his own comfort and consolation and — here was the beauty of it — the sweet dream and consolation of millions of Americans.

In his book about the 1984 campaign, *Visions of America*, William A. Henry III wrote: "Reagan's America was a remembered America and, moreover, one remembered not from skeptical scholarly histories but from that psychic attic of imagery in which purple mountain majesties, amber waves of grain, small-town schoolmarms, the cavalry riding to the rescue, Norman Rockwell Thanksgivings, the flag-raising at Iwo Jima, the

World Series, and astronauts landing on the moon somehow seemed interlinked because they each in turn have evoked a swelling sense of personal participation in national pride and purpose."

During the eighties television advertising — Reagan's medium, his art form — perfected a style of all-American imagery that tapped into Reagan's idealized golden America. Reagan and American advertising labored in a sort of unconscious concert to recrystallize an American self-image that had been shattered by a procession of traumas that began with John Kennedy's assassination.

But Americans have their private landscapes as well, American memories not yet dispensed by the chain stores. America is only what each of us knows.

I spent much time on the Chesapeake Bay in Maryland when I was a child. My great grandfather owned an island in the bay — Cobb Island. He won it in a poker game. He built a summer house on the island — a slightly eccentric Victorian house with, here and there, turrets that seemed to make no sense, and a porch that veered off at an unexpected angle.

The island was heavily wooded in those days, and could be reached from the mainland only by sailboat or skiff. No one else lived on the island. My grandmother — my father's mother — spent idyllic summers there as a child around the turn of the century. She had her own sailboat and horses. I carry in my mind a snapshot of her as an adolescent girl in broad-brimmed turn-of-the-century sun hat and ankle-length skirt, standing in a field beside the bay on Cobb Island in a sun-dazed light.

I did not see Cobb Island until more than fifty years later, when my father drove me there one Sunday when I was an adolescent. The island had become a densely populated summer colony, reached by causeway from the mainland. The old house was still there, however, and my father looked at it wonderingly. His grandfather had sold it years before.

The Chesapeake Bay, in any case, has a sort of dreamy significance in my mind, and perhaps in the collective unconscious of my family. I went to the bay often as a child—boating and sailing and swimming there, being stung by the jellyfish.

I have been becalmed on its shallow glassy waters on motionless hot summer afternoons—the calm followed in an hour or two by a moment when the sky turned an ominous copper color, and the haze coagulated to an angry density, and at last the summer storm banged down with lashing rain and winds that tore violently at the sails until we had clawed them down the mast.

So the sight of the Chesapeake Bay (we always called it *the* Chesapeake Bay, not Chesapeake Bay, as it is correctly known) stirs in me associations of familiarity and longing and, more obscurely, of heartbreak. That last is somewhat difficult to explain, or even to understand. I often feel about American landscapes—especially those that mean the most to me—a sense of exhilaration and recognition that is accompanied by a melancholy, a note of elegy. That is my own temperament perhaps.

West Texas, for example, has that somewhat haunted quality in my imagination. The vibration is of something lost and not to be regained. Maybe it is simply the past itself, and the fact that the past hangs around places, haunting them a little and being, by definition, something gone.

The American landscape is new, various, exuberant, but it also has its ghosts, its afterlives. Which is not to say that such landscapes are depressing. A place that has had, so to speak, a prior life is exhilarating. It communicates meanings and suggests mysteries about itself that raw newness cannot give. The poignance of many American landscapes derives from the way the haunted meanings coexist with the sleek and hopeful violence of the new.

One sees the effect all the time in the American South, the South being, of all American regions, the most haunted.

When I was six or seven years old I spent a summer on my Uncle Bernard's tobacco farm outside Winston-Salem, North Carolina. Uncle Bernard and Aunt Gertrude were vigorous Methodists with many daughters and one son, their youngest child, Jim. Their farm, which lay in gently hilly pastureland and pine woods, was given over to dairy cows, and to corn and tobacco. Uncle Bernard's family lived in a sturdy farmhouse that was painted green and white, I think. It stood at the end of a long dirt road that led, in a mile or so, to another dirt road and thence, somewhere beyond, to the two-lane blacktop that went to Winston-Salem and Raleigh and Durham and the rest of civilization.

A gliding couch swing stood on the broad front porch. As punishment for our misdemeanors, which were many, my older brother and I were often locked in our upstairs bedroom. We climbed out the window and across the roof of that porch, and jumped to the branch of an overhanging tree. We shinnied down and were gone for the rest of the day into the North Carolina countryside.

We learned to be careful there. Uncle Bernard often killed copperheads and rattlesnakes out in the woods and fields. My brother and I often escaped to our favorite swimming hole, a wide deep place in the creek where the cows sometimes came to water. The swimming was given an extra thrill of fear by the knowledge that water moccasins lived there.

One day when we escaped from the upstairs room where we had been locked, my brother and I set off through the pine woods, and at length came upon a dirt road that we knew. Uncle Bernard had taken us along that road in his mule-drawn wagon, holding the reins loosely and clucking at the mules to keep them going, and calling "gee!" or "haw!" to the animals, speaking their language, telling them which way to go.

Now the road was empty. There is a loneliness like abandonment on an empty, sun-washed, dusty southern road. We felt it, and at length we veered off among the pines again, keeping the road in sight, but pretending to reconnoiter.

In half an hour we heard noises — voices, clanking metal — and crept toward them, keeping low in the pines. I had never seen a chain gang before. Black men in striped prison clothes were working on the road with picks and shovels. White men in uniforms and broad-brimmed hats stood guard. Each held a shotgun cradled easily in the crook of an arm, or else stood with the gun butt propped in the tuck of the waist just above the hipbone with the barrel pointed skyward at an angle.

The white guards ordered the black men here and there with an easy conversational menace. My brother and I watched for a time, unseen and silent, then slipped off into the deeper woods.

Landscapes bring back whatever has occurred upon them, within them. Remembering North Carolina that day, I think of a poem by Robert Penn Warren (whose instruments have always been well-tuned to the resonances of American places) called "Pondy Woods." The poem is about a fugitive slave, chased through pine woods by white men with bloodhounds. It begins: "The buzzards over Pondy Woods achieve blue, tense altitudes,/ Drifting high in the pure sunshine/ til the sun in gold decline. . . ."

I did not think of North Carolina as an evil landscape. I was not at an age when one makes such moral judgments anyhow. But the place impressed itself deeply upon my memory, and thereby acquired that mythic prior life that comes back to me whenever I travel in the South.

I see the images of the landscape with a dreamy clarity. A large white farmer in white straw hat and bib overalls and ankle-high lace-up work boots leaves his pickup truck and walks across a field of young tobacco toward a distant tree. A black man has been lying under the tree, but rises swiftly when he sees the white farmer approach. The white farmer comes upon the black man, and just as the black man tries to dodge away, the white man aims a hard kick that lands on the black man's backside. But since the black man was moving away, the kick causes him only to stagger a little. He recovers his balance and stands shuffling between two rows of short tobacco plants. The white farmer points abruptly, stabbing his arm at full length like a rifle aimed at the distance, and thus aims the black man at that distant target. The black man goes off in that direction, as told. The white farmer struts back to his pickup with satisfied eyes.

Uncle Bernard's son Jim was sixteen that summer. He rode a pinto pony like a cowboy across the cow pastures, riding at a full gallop. One day Jim took his father's twelve-gauge shotgun out into the pasture. I did not know why—to shoot at birds, perhaps. From a distance of fifty yards or so, I watched Jim as he stood in profile to me in the middle of the pasture, the dense cowpats all around his feet. I had never seen a gun fired at a distance before. I saw the gun's muzzle emit a puff of smoke, silently. A dream. And then, after the longest moment, there came the *boom!* of the report. Reality had been torn asunder—sight and sound cracked off from one another in a fissure I could not comprehend. That territory, North Carolina, has remained in memory, surreal and magic and ominous.

I return often to the Florida Keys, which have for me a brighter kind of magic. I spent two months there one spring when I was eight years old. I was astonished then that the Keys were a part of the United States. I had been plucked out of Washington, D.C., which was still ice-patched and gray in early spring, its air biting and its trees bare, and had been transported down the Atlantic coast to an American antiworld full of dazzling colors and a humid air I had never felt before — close and sexual, though I could not have put it in those terms.

The American sense of place in the Keys, in Key West, remains strong, although each time I return another stretch of the causeway has been widened to four lanes, and more of the coral is covered with new hotels and condominiums.

When I was in Key West as a child, it was a brawlingly masculine town. Sailors from the naval base threw one another through the plate-glass windows of the hotels downtown on Saturday nights. Smugglers and fishermen drank in dives down near the harbor. The spirit of Ernest Hemingway still presided, although he had already divorced his second wife, Pauline Pfeiffer, and decamped with his third wife, Martha Gellhorn, to Cuba.

Eventually, Key West became a writer's colony and a heavily homosexual resort — another American transformation. Its sense of place remains strong. It is interesting to watch a place change its gender — or at least its clientele — and find that you love it as much as you did.

I go bonefishing in the Keys whenever I can. I do not care about the fish I catch so much as the colors of the water out on the bone flats — turquoises and blues and greens and purples and aquamarines — and the moodworks of the water as it is altered by the passages of clouds and wind, and, beneath the surface, the sliding and darting of barracuda and manta rays and sharks and snapper and all of that teeming life.

I am ten years old. My canoe slides, just after dawn, across Saranac Lake in the Adirondack Mountains. Two feet above the water hangs a layer of wisping fog. The brown water is glass-smooth, and the canoe cuts through it with a sweet precision, the V of ripples parting from the bow like the beginning of the world.

The lake is swampish, and old stumps rise out of the water, like ruins, like broken columns: the landscape of the primordial combines weirdly with an intimation of aftermath. The morning fills me with a sense of the miraculous. I rest my paddle now across the gunwales, and the canoe slips forward, frictionless, across the smooth water.

A kingfisher, the only sign of life in the swamp, stands upon a stump in the fog. Then fires off through the stillness like an electron.

Perhaps it is the America one remembers from childhood that remains forever resonant in one's mind. But that is not it either. One can be haunted in different ways.

In the late 1960s I flew to Santa Fe, New Mexico, and spent a morning hanging around a general store on the edge of town. I was looking for an entrée to one of the communes then operating in the surrounding wilderness. I wanted to find one called Morningstar.

The utopian impulse had swept across America in those days, although utopianism implies a serenity often absent in those militant times. The communes were frequently beset. They turned into fortresses.

In midmorning I began talking to a cheerful backpacking long-haired young man from California who was buying bags of rice and grain with food stamps. I learned that he came from Morningstar. I asked if I could give him a ride back up there in my rental car, and perhaps walk into the mountains to talk to the others.

We drove into the Sangre de Cristo Mountains to the north. The mountains unfolded in numinous hazed-blue layers, and they did seem haunted indeed, although with mysteries quite distant from anything that my childhood in the East had taught me — Indian mysteries, pantheisms.

The boy from California had run away from home and was on the road, as so many of the American young were in those days. He was, nonetheless, cheerful, and frisky as a young dog. We left the car in a clearing by the road halfway up a mountain, and then walked up a rocky trail through stunted pine.

I had heard stories about the state of siege. Racial and class hatreds buzzed through these mountains now. The poor Chicanos and Indians hated the hippies, who lived on food stamps and trust funds, and took up a mock poverty that affronted the truly poor. There were rapes, it was said. Shots were fired. The hippies in the communes kept themselves armed with .30–.30 rifles. Some of them were in these mountains for the purpose of staying drugged on mescaline and peyote and LSD, and the thought of one of them staring down a gunsight at me through the trees in a state of chemical enlightenment made me twitchy. I walked up the trail with my palms upraised and spread before me in a relaxed way, like a priest in benediction at the end of a low mass.

No one fired. We came at last into a small village of low-rise hovels. The commune. My young guide, the frisking dog, led me eagerly to one of the hovels—a log-walled dugout with a sloping and incompetent roof. We opened the canvas door flap and stepped inside. It took a moment for my eyes to become accustomed to the darkness.

Around a dying fire sat five or six young white men, wearing long hair and beards and filthy clothes. They were not glad to see me. They answered my questions in grunts. Three of them were obviously stoned. I talked to them for a little while, but found myself enormously depressed by them, and walked outside.

They had gone back to American nature—not back, really, since they had never been there before. They did not understand it, and they were too stoned even to be sentimental about it. Their women did all the work, drawing water from a spring a quarter of a mile down the trail, and searching for firewood, just like the women of the Masai.

I inspected the garden where they had tried farming. One of them in a bucolic mood had taken a sharp stick and scratched the earth and thrown some seeds unavailingly at the soil. O pioneers!

But the countryside was lovely and magic. The Americans in this case had not risen to the occasion.

The landscapes come into one's life randomly, and then become part of it and of one's memory. Large landscapes, perhaps, encasing small incidents.

One afternoon when I was fifteen years old I was walking down a logging trail in the Great Smokey Mountains of Tennessee. The Smokeys have a shaggy power about them. They seemed to me to be the stage at which the sweeter and more genteel slopes of the Virginia mountains, the Blue Ridge and the Shenandoah Valley, turned into something a little more serious, and took on something of the southern sinister.

My friends and I were several hours' hike from the nearest paved road. We walked on a crude path cut through stands of the deepest woods. Suddenly a man stepped out from behind a large pine tree. He wore overalls and a slouch hat, much weathered.

We stopped and looked at him questioningly.

"Y'all boys want to turn around and go the other way, now," he told us, his voice not friendly but coming across to us on a dead flat trajectory.

I did not understand at first. One of my friends who was older than I looked at the man, and said, just as flatly, "Yes."

A simple encounter in the picturesque American landscape. One did not quarrel with the territorial rights of moonshiners in those mountains. We turned and stepped back down the fire road, and when I looked again, the moonshiner had vanished into the woods.

One of my favorite American rivers is the Susquehanna, a broad, graceful river that goes sleeping down through Pennsylvania. When I was sixteen and seventeen years old, I worked during the summers for a daily newspaper in a small town on the banks of the Susquehanna. I lived in a boarding house just a block from the river. I was lonely, and in the evenings sometimes I would walk to the riverbank and watch the handsome sweep of the river as the sun receded.

There were many islands in the river, abundantly wooded, and they pleasingly broke the evening light that glinted on the water as the sun went down — dark tufts on the glistening stream of light. The river stirred me. It heightened my sense of loneliness — a dramatic adolescent loneliness.

Danville, the small town on the Susquehanna, bore only the slightest resemblance to the small-town America of Ronald Reagan's nostalgia.

It was a nice town. I ate at the Greek restaurant on Main Street, and on Friday nights, the undertaker's son and I and a few other blades of Montour County would pile into the undertaker's hearse with a few six-packs of beer, and drive up the highway to see the drive-in movie in Bloomsburg, the home of the state teacher's college.

A state mental hospital stood on the edge of town. My landlady, a tough little Welsh widow, had been a nurse there for years. There was a chemical plant, which employed many of the townspeople, and a large, first-class medical center. To the west lay open farm country. To the north and east lay the Pennsylvania coalfields, an infinitely grimier and sadder region. Sometimes I drove there to cover a story for the *Danville News*.

I hated the coal region. Everything in the towns — everything in nature itself — was begrimed. If one walked the pavement, one fairly slid on a fine black powder. The children were begrimed, and when I talked to them I sometimes thought that they would never escape and were damned.

Americans never like to think of their children in that way. No one does. But for Americans the thought creates an ideological dissonance.

When I left the coal-region towns, I fled back to the Susquehanna and crossed to the other side as if I were departing an underworld — as of course I was.

Nothing happened. A farmer's leg was crushed when his tractor rolled on him. A confidence man tried to sell stolen cars at the car auction, and he was caught. Dwight Eisenhower sent Marines to Lebanon. A car flew off the highway one night in the fog and landed in a ravine, and everyone was killed. I took the report over the telephone from the state police and wrote a story. I sat in my room and wrote love letters and read the landlady's Presbyterian magazines, with their news of the far-off missions.

The Susquehanna River was lovely, but Danville was the most flatly unresonant American town that I have known. If Danville had a soul, a quality that was distinctly its own, if Danville had a meaning to be gotten at, it escaped me.

Although Danville did not lend itself to being idealized, it was surely American, and one would find there, when winter came, the recumbent figure of a father passed out on the porch in the cold, that side of America that Ronald Reagan effaced, as a boy would.

The American trajectories officially fire forward. But the American mind also goes back and back, reaching for something — sometimes something that is not there.

Henry David Thoreau had a haunting line: "I long ago lost a hound, a bay horse, and a turtle dove, and I am still on their trail."

Or else Robert Lowell: "Main Street's shingled mansards and square white frames/ date from Warren G. Harding back to Adams./ old life! America's ghostly innocence."

*An abandoned farmhouse in Kansas
looks as though Dorothy just left it for
Oz. In reality many farms, like the inner
cities, have become landscapes of lost
dreams.*

Previous pages: *In this rugged land-scape, now the Canyon de Chelly National Monument, the Navajos made their last stand against Kit Carson, who forced them into submission by starvation and invasion.*

Left above: *The graceful curves of St. John the Baptist Ukrainian Catholic Church's Byzantine domes soften the stark Pittsburgh skyline.*

Left below: *Founded by the Franciscans in 1786, the mission at Santa Barbara, California, was one of many small Spanish settlements where Indians were instructed in Christianity.*

Right: *The Carson Mansion in Eureka, California, built by William Carson, a lumberman and banker in 1850, is a fine example of the Victorian architecture of the period.*

Left: *A grim industrial wasteland in South Chicago.*

Right: *Fierce-looking native wooden sculpture, Hawaii.*

Previous pages: *The swamps of Louisiana are home to the Cajuns, descendants of the Acadians of New Brunswick and Nova Scotia. Driven here by the British troops in the 1750s, they settled along the bayous and continued to regard themselves as a separate people with a unique culture.*

Left: *Traffic in New York City flows in a river of lights.*

Right: *A profusion of signs in San Francisco's Chinatown, the world's largest Chinese community outside Asia. Brightly colored shops, restaurants and other buildings stretch eight blocks along lively Grant Avenue east of Nob Hill.*

GOLDEN
DRAGON

金
龍

NIVERSAL
CAFE
INE CHINESE FOODS

裹球酒家

新
杏
香

樓酒

ING

CHAT HAI

玉器

SUN HUNG HEUNG
CHINESE
CUISINE

of
china
lounge

CHEUNG
RY C

Left: *Wabash Avenue in Chicago with the elevated railway that forms the "Loop" around the downtown core.*

Above: *Totem poles were carved and painted by the Indians of the Pacific Northwest to depict real and mythical animals.*

A sight straight from the 1800s when paddleboats ruled the Mississippi River. These mighty waters have inspired songs and stories and have carried people and cargo up and down the heartland of America.

Below: *Fishing boat on Lake Superior. This massive lake, the world's largest body of fresh water, was called Lake Gitche Gumee by the Chippewa Indians. French explorers found it while looking for a route to the Pacific.*

Right: *Colorful houses in Ketchikan, often called the Gateway to Alaska. This city is the first port of call for ships sailing up the Inside Passage. Fishing boats, pleasure craft and tourist ferries ply the water along its shores.*

Left: *A ribbon of highway connects the Florida Keys, a group of small islands or reefs that stretch from the tip of Florida into the Gulf of Mexico.*

Previous pages: *Katmai National Monument in Alaska is an area of active volcanoes. The Katmai glaciers began to form in 1912 when snow first fell into a newly formed volcanic crater, now a lake.*

Right: *Green and inviting, the vineyards of California produce the state's most valuable crop—its grapes, which are sold all over the country and are made into wines.*

Below: *Parched and dry, the salt flats left behind when the water evaporates crack in the hot dry climate of Utah, leaving an arid and desolate landscape.*

Along much of the California coastline,
steep cliffs rise from the pounding surf.

Right: *Plastic flamingos are often seen decorating lawns and clothing. The real ones are found in the Florida Keys. Their bright plumage and ungainly appearance make them instantly recognizable.*

Above: *An idyllic setting provided by a sheep ranch in Oregon. The state is noted for its mild climate and striking scenery.*

Previous pages: *Famous for its European charm, the French Quarter of New Orleans attracts many visitors eager to see its distinctive buildings and hear its music.*

Right: *The warm waters and sweeping shore of Miami Beach lure many people looking for a break from the cold and hectic pace of the north.*

Left: *The dappled light of spring brings forth the blooms of the apple trees and the dandelions in a profusion of white and yellow.*

Below: *Crystal clear skies and snowy peaks of the Cascade Mountains, a mountain range that stretches from Canada to northern California.*

Right: *Scalding water and hissing stream erupt from beneath the ground at Yellowstone National Park. Geysers are another reminder of the instability of the earth's crust.*

Above: *The other-worldly panorama of Hawaii Volcanoes National Park. All the Hawaiian Islands were formed by volcanic action and some of the craters are still active.*

Left: *Bright splashes of color at Soho, New York. The city's art-colony neighborhood is crammed with galleries, boutiques and stalls. Its name is an acronym for South of Houston Street.*

Previous pages: *Los Angeles has been described as a hundred suburbs in search of a city. Since the city is so spread out and lacks a good public transit system, its inhabitants depend almost entirely on automobiles, leaving the area's expressway system clogged with cars and hazy with exhaust fumes.*

Below: *Bundled up against the cold on historic Salem Street in Boston. The city is one of the country's oldest, known as the cradle of liberty.*

The 375-member choir of the Mormon
Tabernacle in Salt Lake City has won
worldwide recognition. The Latter Day
Saints (Mormons) have long been active
in promoting music and the arts.

The churning sea at Point Lobos, California. The waters that surround America are as much a part of the country's landscape as the mountains and plains.

Right: *Their long history and gentle surroundings give New England towns a special charm.*

Below: *Mt. Rainier seems to hang suspended above the city of Seattle. At over 14,000 feet, the peak is the highest in the state. Its volcanic core gives off fumes, but has not erupted for years.*

Gleaming white in the brilliant sun, adobe buildings like this church are ideally suited to the Southwest. The Pueblo Indians and the Mexicans covered their buildings with mud which dried in the sun. Modern adobe structures are covered with stucco.

These fishing-canning factories in Monterey, California, inspired John Steinbeck to write Cannery Row. *Fish are no longer processed here, but the name Steinbeck gave and the fame he bestowed have preserved the buildings, now used for boutiques, shops and restaurants.*

Left: *A surreal blur of color. Los Angeles at dusk.*

Previous pages: *It took one billion years for the Colorado River to carve the Grand Canyon, one of the most spectacular geological features of the world. The steep walls are predominantly red, but contain a whole spectrum of color.*

Above: *The light of the setting sun sets old and new Atlanta to glowing.*

Right: *The Flatiron Building at Fifth Avenue and Broadway in New York was one of the city's first skyscrapers, built in 1902. Its original name, the Fuller Building, was soon forgotten in favor of its descriptive nickname.*

Previous pages: *The barren expanses of Death Valley, parts of which are below sea level, have earned their ominous name.*

Above: *A sweep of delicate flowers brings a gentle touch to rugged mountain scenery.*

The rugged and wind-thrashed landscape of Big Sur, along the jagged
shoreline of California, has attracted
settlers since 1850. In the 1950s Henry
Miller, Jack Kerouac and others of the
Beat Generation made the area famous
as an artists' and writers' colony.

Left: *The warm glow over Los Angeles is not as inviting as it looks. It is caused in part by pollution from factories and exhaust from cars.*

Right: *Nantucket, Massachusetts, was once one of the greatest whaling centers in the world, used by over a hundred whaling ships. It is now a summer resort, famous for its pleasant climate and striking scenery.*

Above: *Beautiful Oahu is the center of life in Hawaii and a major tourist attraction. The Hawaiian Islands, originally called the Sandwich Islands, were annexed in 1898, and became the fiftieth state in 1959.*

Right: *The old and the new: The ornate Old Court House contrasts vividly with the clean lines of the Renaissance Center, Detroit's tallest building.*

Below: *Endless and arid, the tundra of Alaska is a cold dry region where trees can't grow. The soil is permanently frozen and supports only lichen and mosses and some flowers.*